SAMUEL JOHNSON

SAMUEL JOHNSON

From the engraving by James Watson
from the oil painting by Sir Joshua Reynolds,
now in the possession of the Duke of Sutherland.

SAMUEL JOHNSON

by Hugh Kingsmill pseud,

Lunn, Hugh Kingsmill

"This world, where much is to be done, and
little to be known . . ."　　　JOHNSON.

NEW YORK

The Viking Press

1934

CONTENTS

TO

HESKETH PEARSON

SAMUEL JOHNSON

❋❋❋❋❋❋❋❋❋❋❋❋❋❋❋❋❋❋❋❋❋❋❋❋❋❋❋

CHAPTER ONE

Johnson's Parents—School and Oxford—Marriage

(1)

"WHEN I survey my past life," Johnson wrote in his old age, "I discover nothing but a barren waste of time, with some disorders of body and disturbances of the mind very near to madness."

His mental disturbances, which did not become acute before his twentieth year, were derived from his father. He had inherited a melancholy from his father, he once said, which had made him mad all his life, or at least not sober. His physical defects were accidental, not inherited, and are explained in his *Annals,* a fragment of an autobiography, the rest of which he burned shortly before his death. When he was a few weeks old, he was put out to nurse. The son of his wet-nurse was short-sighted and scrofulous, and both these complaints soon developed in the baby Johnson. It is clear that he was infected by his nurse's milk. Johnson records that this was the opinion of his godfather, Dr. Swinfen, and adds without comment that his mother thought his disease derived from her family. It was no doubt to lessen her remorse over her baby's condition that she attributed it to an hereditary taint and not to the nurse in whose charge she had placed him.

"In ten weeks," he says, "I was taken home, a poor diseased infant, almost blind."

The results of this infection afflicted Johnson throughout

3

his life, his sight and hearing being permanently impaired, and the lower part of his face disfigured by scars. In society he was subject to what his stepdaughter, Lucy Porter, called "convulsive starts and odd gesticulations which tended to one's surprise and ridicule"; and though the cause of these has been disputed, it seems natural to suppose that they were due to the corrosion of his nervous system by the scrofula. These peculiarities of manner were so extraordinary that even those most familiar with him remained keenly conscious of them, while strangers could for some time see nothing else. A characteristic first impression is given by Thomas Campbell, an Irish clergyman, who met Johnson when Johnson was in his sixty-sixth year. "He has the aspect of an Idiot," Campbell wrote in his diary, "without the faintest ray of sense gleaming from any one feature—with the most awkward garb, and unpowdered grey wig, on one side only of his head—he is for ever dancing the devil's jig, and sometimes he makes the most driveling effort to whistle some thought in his absent paroxysms."

Of something more significant in Johnson's appearance than these peculiarities, we might have remained ignorant, had not Mrs. Thrale once written a description of him which ends with these remarkable words: "His sight was near, and otherwise imperfect; yet his eyes were so wild, so piercing, and at times so fierce, that fear was, I believe, the first emotion in the hearts of all his beholders." This glimpse of the man who was concealed from most persons by external oddities is the more striking because it is at variance with Mrs. Thrale's conscious view of Johnson as an unemotional philosopher, and records her spontaneous intuition of the lifelong struggle which he fought in defence of his mental and emotional balance. Of the odds against him in this struggle, the earliest to reveal itself, and perhaps the most complex in its after-results, was his infantile infection, the outward signs of which provoked such derision among relatives and strangers alike.

The responsibility for the choice of the wet-nurse Johnson assigns to his father. His mother, whom he loved, he tries to exonerate from all suspicion of carelessness. She visited him every day, he says, and even left her fan or glove behind to have an excuse for returning again, but never discovered any signs of neglect. It is impossible to reconcile this apology with the fact that the nurse's son was diseased, and that within a few weeks the baby Johnson almost lost his sight, unless one assumes that Mrs. Johnson had a better heart than head. This inference is supported by Johnson's own account of her, for his love of her did not blind him to the narrowness of her intelligence and her petty outlook on life. In her *Anecdotes of Johnson,* Mrs. Thrale, who drew more intimate confidences from him than anyone else, narrates on his authority that his mother, as the daughter of a small country gentleman, used to make her husband, who was a bookseller, feel his social inferiority. She would worry him, too, with her anxieties over money, but as she knew nothing about business, her laments were equally vague and irritating. Had his mother been more literate, she would have been a better companion to her husband, Johnson says. Although he loved his mother and did not care for his father, his innate fairness of mind made him assign to his mother the greater share of the blame for the joyless married life of his parents. His own matrimonial experience may have strengthened his view that married happiness is more often impaired by the wife than by the husband, but his opinions on marriage seem to have been chiefly shaped by his early memories of his parents. When any matrimonial disputes were brought to his notice, Mrs. Thrale records, Johnson always sided with the husband, whom, he would say, the woman had probably provoked so often that she would long since have forgotten how their dissensions first began. "Women," he said, "give great offence by a contemptuous spirit of non-compliance on petty occasions. The man calls his wife to walk with him in the shade, and she feels a strange desire just at that moment to sit in the sun; he offers to read her a play, or sing her a song, and she calls the children in to disturb them, or advises him to seize that opportunity of settling the family accounts. . . . Are the hours of pleasure so frequent in life, that when a man gets a couple of quiet ones to spend in familiar chat with his wife, they must be poisoned by petty mortifications?"

The reference to children in this passage is particularly applicable to Johnson's parents, who married late in life and had far more pleasure from their offspring than from each other. Michael Johnson was fifty-three, his wife forty, when their first child, Samuel, was born on September 18, 1709. The character of Michael Johnson can be gathered from stray passages in his son's *Annals* and in Mrs. Thrale's *Anecdotes*. Though lacking in business aptitude, and increasingly embarrassed for money as his life advanced, he must have had abilities above the average, for he rose to be a magistrate of Lichfield, the Staffordshire town where he worked at his trade of selling books. That he had much of his son's love of books for their own sakes is shown by a remarkable reference to him in a letter written from Trentham in 1716 by the chaplain to Lord Gower: "Johnson, the Litchfield Librarian, is now here; he propagates learning all over this diocese, and advanceth knowledge to its just height; all the clergy here are his pupils, and suck all they have from him."

This tribute to Michael Johnson's union of learning and piety would lead us to expect a close sympathy between him and his eldest son. Yet Johnson always spoke of his father with a coldness not far removed from aversion. He described him to Mrs. Thrale as pious and worthy, but wrong-headed, positive, and melancholy; and added that it was only the long journeys on horseback which his father took in the course of business that preserved his sanity. The combination of positiveness and melancholia in the elder Johnson would not in themselves account for his son's lack of affection, exasperating though one's own faults or weaknesses are when reflected in a parent or a child. It was the petty scale on which Michael Johnson's positiveness asserted itself that disgusted his son. Like many men who are ineffectual in the outside world, Michael Johnson was consequential and self-assertive at home, laying a ban on tea as too expensive, and discouraging his wife from paying or receiving visits. Johnson narrates how once, when his father came to fetch him and his younger brother from their aunt's house in Birmingham, he told the ostler that he had twelve miles home and two boys under his care. This offended Johnson. There seems small cause for offence in this episode. But Johnson had a hatred of pretentiousness which blinded him even as a grown man to its pathetic side. He was ten when this incident occurred, and if one pictures Michael assuming the air of a Cæsar about to cross the Rubicon, the ostler grinning sardonically, and young Samuel writhing in the agony which children feel when their parents are making fools of themselves, one can understand the lasting impression this trivial scene made upon him.

Michael was proud of his son's intelligence, which showed itself at a very early age, but it was his own vanity, not a disinterested pleasure in his child's powers, which was gratified. Johnson soon learned to dislike his father's caresses, because he knew that he was being petted into a willingness to show off his cleverness before strangers, and used to run out of the house, when visitors arrived, and climb up a tree. "The great misery of late marriages," he once said, "is that the unhappy produce of them becomes the plaything of dotage: an old man's child leads much such a life, I think, as a little boy's dog, teized with awkward fondness, and forced to sit up and beg . . . to divert a company, who at last go away complaining of their disagreeable entertainment."

If he seems too harsh to his father, it should be remembered that the traces of his infantile malady must have been particularly marked in his childhood, so that the natural shyness of children before strangers would have been heightened in him almost to a panic. Later, when he learnt that his father was responsible for the choice of his nurse, his disgust at the insensitiveness which allowed him to parade his disfigured child before strangers would be intensified.

His dislike of his father turned all his early affection towards his mother, for whose favour he used to compete with his younger brother Nathanael. Nathanael, who died in his late twenties, once complained that Samuel scarcely treated him with common civility. Johnson's feeling that he was entitled on all occasions to preferential treatment, one of his most marked characteristics, was strengthened by his mother's spoiling of him, for she indulged him as far as her poverty allowed, partly no doubt to make up to him for his ill-health. This spoiling was so agreeable to him that, when he looked back on it in after-life, he quite forgot his usual severity as a moralist, and used to urge the importance of conciliating children by kindness, once saying that he would never have loved his mother so in later years, had she not given him coffee she could ill afford, to gratify his appetite when a boy.

A pathetic story which Boswell tells, in his life of Johnson, will satisfy rigid disciplinarians that Mrs. Johnson over-indulged Samuel's moods as well as his appetites, and will illustrate for others how sensitive he was to his physical defects from his earliest years. One day when the servant who used to be sent to conduct him home from school had not come in time, he set out by himself, though he was then so near-sighted that he was obliged to stoop down on his hands and knees to get over the gutter. His school-mistress, afraid that he might miss his way, or be run over by a cart, followed him. He happened to turn round and see her, and, running at her in a rage, beat her as well as his strength would permit.

More than sixty years later, when Dr. Percy, with as little intention of offending as this school-mistress, reminded Johnson that he was short-sighted, Johnson, after a preliminary insult which Dr. Percy resented, fell upon him with the same fury he had shown against his teacher: "Hold, Sir! Don't talk of rudeness; remember, Sir, you told me (puffing hard with passion struggling for a vent) I was short-sighted. We have done with civility. We are to be as rude as we please." But the storm died down as quickly as it had arisen. "Percy: Upon my honour, Sir, I did not mean to be uncivil. Johnson: I cannot say so, Sir; for I *did* mean to be uncivil, thinking you had been uncivil."

Another proof of his mother's solicitude for him is her journey to London, when he was two and a half, to have him touched by Queen Anne, for the royal touch was in those days believed to be efficacious against his malady. The expense of the journey worried her greatly: she went to London in a coach, but, to save a few shillings, returned in a wagon, giving as her excuse his violent cough, which she feared might annoy their fellow-travellers in the coach. So their fellow-travellers in the wagon had to suffer instead. "We were troublesome to the passengers," Johnson says. "I was sick; one woman fondled me, the other was disgusted."

These scraps of memory were written down by Johnson in the sickness and solitude of his old age, to console him with the recollection of his poor mother's love and to charm him with the magic in which time clothes even the most trivial or wretched details of the past. On this journey to London, he records, his mother bought him a small silver cup and a spoon, and had them marked "Sam. I.," fearing that if they were marked "S. I.," her own initials, they might be taken from him after her death. She also bought him a speckled linen frock, which he always referred to as "my London frock." The spoon, he writes, was still in his possession, but his wife had sold the cup in the worst days of their poverty— "the cup was one of the last pieces which dear Tetty sold in our distress."

Thirty-eight pages are missing from the *Annals,* between his visit to London and his first days at school, to which the last surviving pages are devoted. The style here is easier, and if there was a progressive relaxation of his customary reserve in the hundreds of later pages which he destroyed, one can infer that he had revealed more of his life and emotions than he could bear the world to know. The complete manuscript may have been the greatest autobiography in our literature, and would certainly, written as it was from the inside by so sincere a man, have given a more truthful and complete picture of Johnson than we now possess.

The even balance which Johnson kept between his love for his mother and his clear sense of her limitations appear again in the last pages. He was once, he writes, very anxious about a piece of school work in which he had failed several times. His mother encouraged him, and he got on better. "When I told her of my good escape, 'We often,' said she, dear mother! 'come off best when we are most afraid.' " She was proud of his quick progress, he continues, and after illustrating her pride, by recalling some words of praise she once gave him, he concludes, "These little memorials soothe my mind." But he also narrates his mother's concern when, during a visit to his Birmingham aunt at the age of ten, he astonished his aunt by eating a vast portion of a boiled leg of mutton. His mother was greatly upset, and told him his greediness would never be forgotten.

The absence in Johnson of the sentiment of filial reverence will surprise those who think of him as a bigoted champion of all established conventions. But it was consistent both with his personal experience and with his general attitude to life. "Poor people's children," he said to Mrs. Thrale, "never respect them: I did not respect my own mother, though I loved her; and one day, when in anger she called me a puppy, I asked her if she knew what they called a puppy's mother." So far from holding that parents are entitled to the gratitude of their children, he maintained that the only special obligation involved in the relationship of parents and children existed on the side of the parents. To have voluntarily become to any being, he wrote in *The Rambler,* the occasion of its existence produces an obligation to make that existence happy. As a corollary to this opinion, he maintained that parents had no rights, merely as parents, over their children. The parent's moral right could arise only from his kindness, and his civil right only from his money. One day when Mrs. Thrale, referring to a passage in Xenophon, praised Cyrus for asking his father's permission to marry, Johnson burst out: "If Cyrus by his conquests had not purchased emancipation, he had conquered to little purpose indeed. Can you bear to see the folly of a fellow who has in his care the lives of thousands, when he begs his papa permission to be married, and confesses his inability to decide in a matter which concerns no man's happiness but his own?"

But the deepest reason for his small respect for parents lay in his preoccupation with the virtue of the individual. His observation of life had shown him that goodness is always rare, and that it is especially rare in the old. Men commonly grew wickeder as they grew older, he once said, and added that he was always on the young people's side when there was a dispute between them and the old ones, for a man had at least a chance of virtue till age had withered its very root.

This view he elaborated in *Rasselas,* in a passage which contrasts youth and age. "The old man pays regard to riches, and the youth reverences virtue. The old man deifies prudence: the youth commits himself to magnanimity and chance. The young man who intends no ill, believes that none is intended, and therefore acts with openness and candour; but his father having suffered the injuries of fraud, is impelled to suspect, and too often allured to practise it. . . ."

This attitude, however strange in a champion of the established order, was natural in a follower of Christ, who, when he was told that his mother and brethren desired to speak to him, pointed to his disciples and said, "Behold my mother and my brethren! For whosoever shall do the will of my Father which is in heaven, the same is my brother, and sister, and mother."

Even Johnson's penance at Uttoxeter, one of the most famous episodes in his life, was rather in expiation of his sin against God in indulging his pride than in expiation of his filial disobedience. He could not in general, he said, accuse himself of having been an undutiful son, but on one occasion he refused from pride to go with his father to Uttoxeter market. Many years later, desiring to atone for this fault, he went to Uttoxeter in very bad weather, and stood for a considerable time bareheaded in the rain, on the spot where his father's stall used to stand. "In contrition I stood, and I hope the penance was expiatory."

(2)

Young Johnson's disease was offset by two great advantages over his schoolfellows—his superiority in brains and in muscle. The extraordinary physical strength which he inherited from his father, and which was trained by a prize-fighting uncle, was useful to him not only as a boy, but contributed throughout his life to his ascendancy over other men. Even in the most civilized surroundings, the feeling that an argument could, if the other man chose, be terminated by his throwing one through the window tempers self-assertion; and in the eighteenth century brute force was more quickly resorted to than today. Johnson often used his strength in his early years in London, and the story of how he thrashed a bookseller, Tom Osborne, became a legend, about which Mrs. Thrale one day begged him to give her the true particulars. "There is nothing to tell, dearest lady," Johnson answered complacently, "but that he was insolent and I beat him, and that he was a blockhead and told of it, which I should never have done; so the blows have been multiplying, and the wonder thickening for all these years. . . . I have beat many a fellow, but the rest had the wit to hold their tongues."

His strength was supported by unusual courage, which he made a practice of testing when an occasion offered. Sir John Hawkins, in his life of Johnson, narrates that after not having swum for many years Johnson went into the river at Oxford, and swam away to a part of it that he had been told of as a dangerous place, and where a man had been drowned. More remarkable was his fight with four men who attacked him one night, and whom he kept at bay till the watch came up, and carried both him and them to the round-house.

One would expect such a man to have been a prodigy even in his youth, and the little we know of Johnson as a boy bears out this expectation. The retort to his mother, already quoted, shows how intractable he was as a child. Nathanael's complaint that Samuel scarcely treated him with common civility suggests the excessively overbearing element in his character before it was modified by his latent goodness of heart; and Sir John Hawkins confirms the impression that he was spoilt and irritable with a picture of him in the house of a Lichfield neighbour. The children of the family, annoyed by his rudeness, used to call him the great boy. The father, once overhearing this, said: "You call him the great boy, but take

my word for it, he will one day prove a great man." Beneath
his physical strength and roughness, this prophecy shows, his
moral and intellectual qualities were already discernible, and
a few years later, when he was in his teens, they were already
so developed as to give him, supported as they were by
physical strength, a strange ascendancy over his schoolfellows.
Edmund Hector, a friend of Johnson's at Lichfield Grammar
School, used to call for him each morning with two other
boys, one of whom took him on his back, while the other two
supported him on each side. This ascendancy is the more remarkable because Johnson did not, like other youthful heroes,
Clive, Napoleon, and du Guesclin, establish his authority by
organizing his schoolfellows in mimic warfare or raids on
property. Now, as later, his domination of others was due to
nothing but his personal qualities. He did not even join with
the other boys in their games, being prevented partly by his
short sight and partly by his constitutional indolence, which
was already remarkable. "A long, lank, lounging boy" is the
description one of his contemporaries used to give of him
in later life; and Edmund Hector told Boswell that Johnson's
chief pleasure was sauntering in the fields with him, "during
which he (Johnson) was more engaged in talking to himself
than his companion." Even when there was a frost, he would
not warm himself by sliding on the ice, but would request
one of his schoolfellows to pull him along by a garter tied
round his waist.

Though he once complained that Hunter, his headmaster
at Lichfield, used to beat the boys unmercifully, Johnson
favoured the rod as a stimulus to effort, and replied to someone who was expressing his pleasure that children were being
less whipped than formerly—"What they gain at one end,

they lose at the other." He approved the rod on moral grounds, too. It produced an effect which terminated in itself. A child was afraid of being whipped, and therefore learned his task, but by exciting emulation and comparisons of superiority the foundation of lasting mischief was laid. Yet his own achievements as a scholar were due more to his desire to excel than to the many thrashings he received from Hunter. Though too indolent to apply himself methodically to his work, he had fits of enormous energy during which he absorbed far more than the others, and the gratification his superiority gave him was not forgotten in later years. "They never," he told Boswell, "thought to raise me by comparing me to anyone; they never said, Johnson is as good a scholar as such a one; but such a one is as good a scholar as Johnson; and this was said but of one, but of Lowe; and I do not think he was as good a scholar."

Intellectual development, so far as it can be distinguished from the other two, is less important than moral and imaginative development. Even as a small boy, Johnson was a moralist, and already divined and feared the temptations of life. Having, he narrates in the *Annals,* read in one of his classical authors that some man, when he hated another, made him rich, he went home and repeated this passage in the hearing of his mother, who, he says, could never conceive that riches could bring any evil. One would not be surprised to learn that it was on this occasion she was so unforeseeing as to call him a puppy.

The imaginative element in Johnson was very strong, and would have made him a great poet, had he been able to harmonize it with the moral element, but the conflict between the two was never resolved. In *Rasselas,* thinking of those expectations of happiness and glory which outstrip what can be realized on earth, he speaks of "that hunger of imagination which preys incessantly upon life." Like Cervantes, he was much given to day-dreaming and the reading of romances. Even in later life, on a visit to Dr. Percy, he spent most of his time reading an enormous Spanish romance in folio, and he would sometimes attribute to this passion the unsettled state of mind which had prevented him from taking up a profession. Here the moralist in Johnson is condemning the poet, but when Mrs. Thrale defended *Goody Two Shoes, Tommy Prudent,* and the other moral tales for children which were coming into fashion in the last half of the eighteenth century, he rebuked her. "Babies do not want to hear about babies," he said; "they like to be told of giants and castles, and of somewhat which can stretch and stimulate their little minds."

It was largely this imaginative strain in Johnson which prevented him from being a scholar in the strict sense. He read voraciously as a boy, his chief period of study being between twelve and eighteen; but he read what his nature needed, and had none of the born scholar's capacity for patient progress along prescribed routes.

At fifteen Johnson left Lichfield for the Grammar School at Stourbridge, where he was on bad terms with the headmaster, Mr. Wentworth. His approval of authority never, from his earliest years, included its application to himself. "Mr. Wentworth," he told Boswell, "was a very able man, but an idle man, and to me very severe; but I cannot blame him much. I was then a big boy; he saw I did not reverence him; and that he should get no honour from me."

From Stourbridge he returned to his father's shop at Lichfield. Michael Johnson hoped to teach his son his own trade. But he was defeated by Samuel's inertia. Apart from his general unfitness for such a life, the romances which were his favourite reading must have disgusted him with the prospect of wasting himself in a shop. His vanity, at any rate in his youth, was humiliated by his low social position, and even in his old age he did not care to talk much of his family. One has little pleasure, he said, in reciting the anecdotes of beggary; and the same distaste is revealed in a letter to Mrs. Thrale, in which he wrote: "Mr. Cornelius Harrison was the only one of my relations who ever rose in fortune above penury, or in character above neglect."

The drudgery in the shop which Samuel declined fell on the shoulders of Nathanael, to whose laborious and unprivileged life and early death some of the sympathy expended on Samuel's youth might in fairness be diverted. Nathanael had, however, the advantage over his brother of a cheerful nature. Johnson used to speak with pride of Nathanael's manly spirit, narrating how one day, when the company were lamenting the badness of the roads, Nathanael inquired where they could be, for he travelled the country more than most people, and had never seen a bad road in his life.

As he would not be a bookseller, Samuel was sent to Oxford, entering Pembroke College at the end of October 1728, when he was nineteen years of age. Carlyle has drawn a melancholy but inaccurate picture of Johnson's humiliating situation as a servitor. Johnson was in fact a commoner, and used to join with the other commoners, Sir John Hawkins relates, in hunting the servitors: "and this they did, with the noise of pots and candlesticks, singing to the tune of Chevy Chase the words in the old ballad: 'To drive the deer with horn and hound.' "

But he was very poor, for he went to Oxford only on a promise of assistance from a school friend, and as this assistance was not forthcoming, and his father could no longer afford the small remittances which had been his sole support, he had to leave after he had been up less than fourteen months. The high spirits which impressed the servitors he hunted and the college tutors he defied were assumed to hide his resentment against life. "Ah, Sir, I was mad and violent," he said to Boswell. "It was bitterness which they mistook for frolick. I was miserably poor, and I thought to fight my way by my literature and my wit; so I disregarded all power and authority."

At Oxford, as at school, he resented discipline: tradition relates that he was generally to be seen lounging at the college gate, with a circle of young students round him, whom he was amusing with his wit, and keeping from their work, if not inciting them to rebellion against the college discipline. Yet even at Oxford he was open to reason and sympathetic treatment, and confessed that the mild expostulations of Dr. Adams, then a junior fellow, and later one of his greatest friends, made him ashamed of himself, though he was too proud to show it. He was, too, however little he benefited from Oxford, gratified to have been there. Shortly before his death, when he was on a visit to Dr. Adams, he met Hannah More, and insisted on escorting her all over his old college. "He would let no one show it me but himself," she narrates. " 'This was my room; this Shenstone's.' Then, after pointing out all the rooms of the poets who had been of his college, 'In short,' said he, 'we were a nest of singing-birds. Here we walked, there we played at cricket.' ''

It was during his Oxford period, when he was at home on vacation, that his latent melancholia first made itself strongly felt. So serious was the attack that his friend Edmund Hector was afraid that it might either impair his intellect or endanger his life. To counteract this attack, Johnson several times walked to Birmingham and back, but found so little relief that he decided to apply to his godfather, Dr. Swinfen, and prepared an account of his condition in Latin. Impressed by the force and lucidity of this statement, Dr. Swinfen showed it round Lichfield, as a proof of his godson's talents, much to Johnson's resentment, which could not have been much allayed by Dr. Swinfen assuring him that his melancholia would probably end in madness.

From this time on, Johnson's life was conditioned by his fear of madness, against which he found, on the physical and mental side, remedies in constant occupation of the mind, a great deal of exercise, and restraint in eating and drinking; and on the spiritual side in prayer. As every handicap, if met with intelligence and resolution, produces counterbalancing benefits, Johnson's fear of insanity immensely strengthened his innate truthfulness and sense of reality, for the lies and illusions which make life more comfortable for ordinary men appeared to him as the first steps towards madness. But while his view of this world was made clearer through the danger which threatened him, the feeling of guilt, of being excluded from happiness, now and in any other state of being, which afflicts the emotionally diseased, warped his otherwise profound sense of an ultimate reality. In his most harmonious moments he believed that perfection existed beyond this

world, and that the conditions of attaining it were proportioned to man's powers, concluding his poem, *The Vanity of
Human Wishes:*

> "Pour forth thy fervours for a healthful mind,
>   Obedient passions, and a will resigned;
>   For love, which scarce collective man can fill,
>   For patience, sovereign o'er transmuted ill;
>   For faith, which panting for a happier seat,
>   Counts death kind Nature's signal for retreat."

But he was often distracted with reasonless terrors, which
embodied themselves in the avenging God of a theology he
would have rejected as childish and savage, had he possessed
perfect mental health.

"I am afraid I may be one of those who shall be damned,"
he said to Dr. Adams, a few months before his death. "What
do you mean by damned?" asked the gentle doctor. "Sent to
hell, Sir," Johnson answered loudly and passionately, "and
punished everlastingly!" "You seem, Sir," Mrs. Adams inter-
posed, "to forget the merits of our Redeemer." "Madam,"
Johnson replied, "I do not forget the merits of my Redeemer;
but my Redeemer has said that He will set some on His right
hand and some on His left." The fears which had tormented
him for more than fifty years, and which he was always struggling to repress, began to overcome him; he mastered them
with a strong effort, and broke off the talk with, "I'll have no
more on't."

(3)

Johnson did not take any decided steps towards making a
living during the two and a half years between Oxford and

his father's death, but lived at home, waiting for work to find him. A letter he wrote to a Mr. Hickman, a few weeks before his father died, strikes almost a Micawber note:

"As I am yet unemployed, I hope you will, if anything should offer, remember and recommend, Sir, your humble servant,
SAM. JOHNSON."

Yet even during this period his ability was recognized in the highest society of Lichfield, partly through the exertions of Dr. Swinfen, who was of a very old Staffordshire family; and he was made much of by a number of important residents, among them Captain Garrick, the father of the actor, and Gilbert Walmsley, Register of the Prerogative Court of Lichfield. How greatly he enjoyed this first experience of good society comes out in the tribute which he paid Gilbert Walmsley towards the close of his life. "I knew him very early; he was one of the first friends literature procured me, and I hope that at least my gratitude made me worthy of his notice. He was of an advanced age, and I was only not a boy, yet he never received my notions with contempt. . . . At this man's table I enjoyed many cheerful and instructive hours, with companions, such as are not often found. . . ."

Michael Johnson died in the December of 1731. In the July of the following year, Johnson, having received only twenty pounds from his father's will, realized that some kind of exertion could no longer be avoided. His first attempt, as an usher in a school at Market Bosworth, in Leicestershire, lasted a very short time. He did not know, he wrote to Edmund Hector, whether it was more disagreeable for him to teach, or for the boys to learn. He was disgusted, too, by the insolence of the patron of the school, Sir Wolstan Dixey, at whose table he had to say grace; and, on receiving an invitation to Birmingham from Hector, threw up the job. Hector was lodging with Warren, the most flourishing bookseller in Birmingham. In those days booksellers were also publishers, and Warren found work for Johnson, printing some essays of his in a paper called *The Birmingham Journal,* and commissioning him to translate *A Voyage to Abyssinia,* by Lobo, a Portuguese Jesuit. The task was completed only through the persistence of Hector, who, having roused his friend with a picture of the misery in which the printer and his family were living owing to the slowness with which Johnson was supplying the copy, used to transcribe the translation as Johnson, lying in bed, read it out. The correction of the proof sheets also devolved upon Hector, to whom Johnson, perhaps remembering his friend's unselfish assiduity with some uneasiness, wrote more than twenty years later: "From that kind of melancholy indisposition which I had when we lived together at Birmingham, I have never been free, but have always had it operating against my health and my life with more or less violence."

The preface to this translation, written when Johnson was only twenty-four, is extraordinarily mature, both in style and thought, and foreshadows those conclusions about life on which his moral and his political philosophy were based. There was neither selfishness nor sentimentality in Johnson's conservatism, which derived from his conviction that this world is not an end in itself, but the testing-ground of a virtue which will be rewarded in another life. Utopia, he believed, never had existed on earth, nor ever would exist, and Utopianism was therefore a crime, because it diverted men with unrealizable hopes from the task of individual self-betterment.

The germ of this attitude is contained in his praise of Lobo's sober narrative: "The Portuguese traveller . . . has amused his reader with no romantic absurdity, or incredible fictions . . . he meets with no basilisks that destroy with their eyes, his crocodiles devour their prey without tears, and his cataracts fall from the rocks without deafening the neighbouring inhabitants. The reader will find here no regions cursed with irremediable barrenness, or blessed with spontaneous fecundity; no perpetual gloom, or unceasing sunshine; nor are the nations here described either devoid of all sense of humanity, or consummate in all private or social virtues. Here are no Hottentots without religious polity or articulate language; no Chinese perfectly polite, and completely skilled in all sciences; he will discover, what will always be discovered by a diligent and impartial inquirer, that wherever human nature is to be found, there is a mixture of vice and virtue, a contest of passion and reason."

The subdued humour and balanced outlook shown in this passage were the reverse side of the passionate and romantic nature which delighted in the old tales of chivalry. But Johnson had no youthful period of love and adventure. His indolence and melancholia hampered his naturally enterprising character, and his strong attraction towards women, which troubled him all his life, was barred from any outlet before his marriage both by his physical disadvantages and by his religious principles. In his twenties he was lean and lank, and the immense structure of his bones was hideously striking to the eye, according to his stepdaughter, Lucy Porter, to whom we are also obliged for the information that his convulsive starts and odd gesticulations excited surprise and ridicule. It was perhaps even more his extreme sensitiveness to contempt than his principles which kept him as strictly virtuous in his youth as Edmund Hector affirms him to have been, for he once told Thrale that he had never tried to please anyone till he was over thirty, thinking the attempt would be useless.

At the house of Gilbert Walmsley, and elsewhere among the gentlefolk of Lichfield, he met, and was attracted by, several young women. But though he put an unusual constraint on his roughness in their presence, he never trusted himself beyond ordinary courtesy. For one of these girls, Molly Aston, Gilbert Walmsley's sister-in-law, he felt the adoration which is inspired by the unattainable. The happiest year of his life, he told Mrs. Thrale, was the one which had been sweetened by a single evening with Molly Aston. "That, indeed, was not happiness, it was rapture," he said. The evening alluded to, Mrs. Thrale is careful to explain, was not passed *tête-à-tête* but in a select company.

Molly Aston had youth, beauty, and good birth. Mrs. Porter, whom Johnson married when he was twenty-five, was twenty years his senior and the widow of a Birmingham tradesman. It might seem at first sight that in despair at the physical defects which prevented him from realizing his youthful dreams of love he resigned himself to someone whose age would make her less fastidious, and who had, at any rate, the solid advantage of a small fortune. Against this simple explanation has to be set Johnson's equally simple statement that it was a love-match on both sides. The truth must lie between these extremes.

Anna Seward, "the Swan of Lichfield," whose admiration and dislike of Johnson were equally violent, mentions more than once that Johnson was in love with Lucy Porter, and only paid his addresses to her mother when Lucy, "disgusted by his ungainly form," rejected him. Anna's memory was sometimes enriched by imagination, and she was always ready to pass on as well-authenticated fact any Lichfield legend which gratified her mixed feelings about "the late stupendous but frail Dr. Johnson," as she once called him. But if this story is true, some pique may at first have been behind Johnson's courtship of Mrs. Porter, though as far as good talk was concerned, Mrs. Porter must have attracted him more than Lucy. Her powers of retort seem on occasion to have been equal to those of Johnson himself, who used to recall with pleasure how, impatient at his constant complaints over the meals she served up, she once interrupted his grace with, "Nay, hold, Mr. Johnson, and do not make a farce of thanking God for a dinner which in a few minutes you will protest not eatable." Even better, if it was ever made, was her reply to Johnson's confession of his disadvantages, when he proposed to her. Anna Seward is our authority for this story, which Boswell rejected on the ground that a very respectable lady of Lichfield, whom Anna had quoted in support of the story, disclaimed any recollection of it.

Johnson, Anna relates, was taken to task by his mother when he broke it to her that he wished to marry a widow almost twice his age. Mrs. Johnson having pointed out that his prospective bride was old, and of extravagant habits, and that he himself was young, poor, and as yet incapable of earning a living, Johnson retorted: "Mother, I have not deceived Mrs. Porter: I have told her the worst of me; that I am of mean extraction; that I have no money; and that I have had an uncle hanged. She replied that she valued no one more or less for his descent; that she had no more money than myself; and that, though she had not had a relation hanged, she had fifty who deserved hanging."

It was doubtless this intellectual sympathy which helped Johnson and Mrs. Porter to overlook each other's disadvantages. Mrs. Porter is reported to have said, soon after they met, that Johnson was the most sensible man she had ever seen. His first impressions of her are not recorded, but though he had perhaps to overcome a certain repugnance to her age, if not to her looks, he may, since he had suffered so much from his physical defects, have considered the unlikelihood that she would bear him children as an additional motive for marrying her. Once started, his courtship would not have been conducted in a despondent spirit. His physical desires were violent; when he was at table he ate with concentrated fierceness until his hunger was allayed, and though he could be abstemious he could not be temperate. Having abstained from sex through the most vigorous years of his life, his passion, as soon as it was encouraged, overwhelmed his taste, which was never discriminating on the æsthetic side, and endowed his bride with beauties not visible to others, and with all the graces possessed by the heroines of his romances. As the one object of his passion, and the chief object of his tenderness, Mrs. Johnson became and remained the centre of his life. More than twenty years after her death, he wrote in his diary, when he was travelling with the Thrales in France: "As I entered (the palace), my wife was in my mind: she would have been pleased. Having now nobody to please, I am little pleased." But that his idealization of her did not obliterate his regret for Molly Aston may perhaps be inferred from a remark he once made about a friend's marriage: "He has done a very foolish thing, Sir; he has married a widow, when he might have had a maid."

The accounts of Mrs. Porter's appearance are conflicting. That she was in her earlier years good-looking above the average is shown by the portrait of her that still exists, and Mrs. Desmoulins, Dr. Swinfen's daughter, said that she was still handsome at the time of her second marriage. Anna Seward's mother, on the other hand, who knew her when she married Johnson, said that she had a very red face and indifferent features, and that her manners had an unbecoming excess of girlish levity and disgusting affectation. David Garrick's description is even less flattering, but Garrick, who was a pupil in the school Johnson ran for a short period after his marriage, had many reasons for resentment against Johnson, and was further tempted to caricature by his powers of mimicry. He used to tell how he and the other boys at Johnson's school took it in turns to look through the keyhole while Johnson was indulging his tumultuous and awkward fondness for Tetty, as he used to call her; and Tetty herself Garrick described as very fat, with swollen, painted cheeks, fantastic in her dress and mincing in her behaviour.

Mrs. Johnson's affectations were a symptom of the same suppressed romanticism which made her husband invest her with imaginary graces. There was, Hawkins says, something crazy in the behaviour of them both—profound respect on his side, and the airs of an antiquated beauty on hers.

They were married on July 9, 1735. On their wedding morning, when they rode together to church, Mrs. Porter was capricious with her lover. "She had read the old romances," Johnson said, "and had got into her head the fantastical notion that a woman of spirit should use her lover like a dog. So, Sir, at first she told me that I rode too fast, and she could not keep up with me; and, when I rode a little slower, she passed me and complained that I lagged behind." Determined not to be made the slave of caprice, he says, he pushed briskly on, and when he at last allowed her to overtake him, she was in tears. This was a favourite story of his, and when he told it to Mrs. Thrale he murmured at the close in tender reminiscence: "Pretty dear creature!"

That Johnson did not wish to touch his wife's money, if any other way of making a living could be found, is shown by his application, a month after his marriage, for the head-mastership of a school at Solihull. Gilbert Walmsley supported his application, which was rejected on two grounds. "All agree that he is an excellent caracter," * wrote Mr. Greswold, the intermediary between Gilbert Walmsley and the trustees of the school, "and on that account deserves much better than to be schoolmaster of Solihull." But, Mr. Greswold continued, Johnson had the reputation of being a very haughty and ill-natured gent, and his way of distorting his face might, it was feared, affect the lads. The "huffing" of the trustees by the late headmaster being still a sore point with them, they were anxious, said Mr. Greswold, not to expose themselves to a second experience of the kind, and must therefore decline the application.

A few months later, Johnson opened a school with his wife's money. "At Edial, near Lichfield, in Staffordshire," the advertisement announced, "young gentlemen are boarded and taught the Latin and Greek languages, by Samuel Johnson." The pupils, who included Captain Garrick's two sons,

* Mr. Greswold's spelling.

David and George, numbered three in all. As Johnson had acquired his own knowledge in spurts, he was ill-qualified, in his own words, "to recall vagrant attention, to stimulate sluggish indifference, and to rectify absurd misapprehension." His appearance, too, was against him with the fathers and mothers of prospective pupils, and after struggling along for over a year without adding to his numbers, he decided to give up his school and try to find work in London as a writer. He was now in his twenty-eighth year.

It was on March 2, 1737, that he left Lichfield for town, accompanied by David Garrick, who had just turned twenty. They carried with them a letter from Gilbert Walmsley to the headmaster of a school at which David was to complete his education before taking up the law. "Davy Garrick," Gilbert Walmsley wrote, "is to be with you next week, and Mr. Johnson to try his fate with a tragedy, and to see to get himself employed in some translation, either from the Latin or the French."

****

CHAPTER TWO

The Struggle for Recognition

(1)

DURING the next twenty-five years of his life, until he received his pension at the age of fifty-two, Johnson was always fighting for enough money to provide necessaries, and was sometimes penniless and without food or lodging. One day in his later years of ease, Mrs. Thrale tells us, he burst into a passion of tears as he was reading out these lines from *The Vanity of Human Wishes:*

> "What ills the scholar's life assail,
> Toil, envy, want, the patron, and the jail.
> See nations slowly wise, and meanly just,
> To buried merit raise the tardy bust."

Had his imagination not been clogged by his melancholia, he would have developed his gifts more easily, and suffered no more and no longer than most men of genius in their struggle for recognition. But the weight on his imagination produced in him, as in Carlyle, an uncertainty of aim. Neither of them was ever quite sure how to employ the genius which he was conscious he possessed. Carlyle used to affirm that a great man can turn his powers with equal effect to any task, and would try to persuade himself that it is pure chance which makes a Shakespeare a poet and not a statesman, or drives a Napoleon to Moscow instead of leaving him to sing in solitude. Johnson, too, managed to persuade himself to this effect: "Those indeed who attain any excellence commonly spend life in one pursuit; for excellence is not often gained upon easier terms. But to the particular species of excellence men are directed, not by an ascendant planet or predominating humour, but by the first book which they read, some early conversation which they have heard, or some accident which excited ardour or emulation."

Hampered in their imaginations, Johnson and Carlyle both began as moralists, for those who are uncertain about themselves find a steadying influence in the instruction of others. Johnson's first work, *Irene,* the tragedy which was in his pocket when he came up to London with Garrick, is simply a versified tract. Less than twenty-five years had elapsed since Addison's tragedy, *Cato,* had been the success of the theatrical season; and on practical as well as on moral grounds Johnson felt that he could not open his London career more auspiciously than by imitating Addison's success. But the capriciousness of fashionable taste had in the meantime found other stimulants than lofty reflections delivered in blank verse, and Johnson's *Irene* was rejected by the manager of Drury Lane, who was concentrating at the moment on pantomimes.

In *Irene* the moralist in Johnson submerged the poet. Addison, Johnson says, employed wit on the side of virtue and religion, and, if the word "wit" is understood to exclude anything amusing, that was also Johnson's aim in his imitation of Addison as a dramatist. Yet, in another mood, he could see the faults of *Cato* clearly, and in his *Life of Addison* objects that the play is "rather a succession of just sentiments and elegant language than a representation of natural affections, or of any state possible or probable in human life. . . . Of the agents we have no care; we consider not what they are doing, nor what they are suffering; we wish only to know what they have to say."

Even this last interest may be faint, if the character has not been made to live by the dramatist's imagination. The supremacy of the imagination merely as a means to conveying moral truths is shown if we compare Macbeth's—

> "I am in blood
> Stepp'd in so far, that, should I wade no more,
> Returning were as tedious as go o'er."

with a variant of the same thought expressed by one of the puppets in *Irene:*

> "Nor think to say, here will I stop,
> Here will I fix the limits of transgression,
> Nor farther tempt the avenging rage of heaven."

While he was putting the final touches to *Irene,* in lodgings at Greenwich, Johnson was considering how to get work from Edward Cave, who, under the name of Sylvanus Urban, owned the best-known periodical of the day, *The Gentleman's Magazine.* Cave, we know both from Johnson and other sources, was a mean employer and an adept in all the mannerisms with which a certain type of newspaper proprietor or publisher makes the literary hack realize how unnecessary he is. When anyone in search of work was shown in to him, he used to remain silent for some minutes, and would then hand his visitor a proof of the forthcoming number of the magazine and ask for his impartial opinion on it. While this was being given, Cave retired into his former abstraction, which increased as his visitor explained the object of his call. If he was interested, he would not betray his interest, but would ask the man to call again, and then astonish him by showing how fully he grasped his proposal.

This was the man whom Johnson relied upon for his chief means of support during several years. He had first written to Cave for work during his Birmingham days, but without success. He wrote again from his Greenwich lodgings, and he finally secured his favour with a Latin Ode, in which he celebrated Cave's disinterested love of literature. Cave was so much pleased with this compliment that he not only printed the Latin version in his magazine, but also two months later an English translation.

Shortly after taking Johnson on to his staff, Cave, in order to bring home to him his privileged position as a contributor to the *Magazine,* requested him to look in one evening at an alehouse in Clerkenwell, where he would see Mr. Browne, one of the *Magazine's* chief writers. Johnson turned up in a loose horseman's coat and a great bushy, uncombed wig, and had the gratification of perceiving Mr. Browne seated at the upper end of a long table, enveloped in a cloud of tobacco smoke. Penniless, and with a wife to support, he had to curb his autocratic temper, and develop his talent for diplomacy, which was greater than is usually supposed.

Having conciliated Cave with the *Ode to Urbanus,* he wrote to him a few days later about a poem called *London,* an imitation of Juvenal's third satire, which he had just composed and which he wanted Cave to recommend to Robert Dodsley, the bookseller. Perhaps because he feared to imperil his chances as a regular contributor if he asked for too much in his own name, he submitted his poem to Cave in such a way as to suggest, without actually stating, that it was the work of another man. "When I took the liberty of writing to you a few days ago," he began, "I did not expect a repetition of the same pleasure so soon; for a pleasure I shall always think it, to converse in any manner with an ingenious and candid man: but having the inclosed poem in my hands to dispose of for the benefit of the author (of whose abilities I shall say nothing, since I send you his performance), I believed I could not procure more advantageous terms from any person than from you, who have so much distinguished yourself by your generous encouragement of poetry; and whose judgement of that art nothing but your commendation of my trifle (*The Ode to Urbanus*) can give me any occasion to call in question. . . . I cannot help taking notice, that, besides what the authour may hope for on account of his abilities, he has likewise another claim to your regard, as he is at present under very disadvantageous circumstances of fortune. . . ."

Dodsley, on Cave's recommendation, agreed to publish the poem, which was immediately successful, going into a second edition within a week. Its theme, the iniquity of London, and the innocent charm of rural existence, was artificial, and peculiarly unsuited to Johnson, who a few years later, writing of his friend Richard Savage's flight to the country, remarked sardonically that Savage "could not bear to lose the opportunity of listening, without intermission, to the melody of the nightingale, which he believed was to be heard from every bramble, and which he did not fail to mention as a very important part of the happiness of a country life."

But though handicapped by an unreal theme, Johnson's vigour makes itself felt in occasional couplets:

> "Here falling hours thunder on your head,
> And here a female atheist talks you dead."

"How, when competitors like these contend,
Can surly virtue hope to fix a friend?"

"This mournful truth is everywhere confess'd,
Slow rises worth by poverty depress'd."

Pope, though the most famous writer and satirist of the day, was delighted by *London,* said that its author would soon be "déterré," and tried to find out something about him, but could discover nothing except his name. Johnson meanwhile was no richer for his success, and his thoughts turned again to schoolmastering. In 1739, the year after *London,* he was offered the headmastership of a school at Appleby, near Lichfield, but the condition was made that he should first obtain his degree as Master of Arts. Dr. Adams tried to persuade Oxford to grant this degree, but was unsuccessful; and Pope, hearing of this attempt, used his influence on Johnson's behalf, though without his knowledge. The details of Pope's effort, supported by Lord Gower, to get Johnson the necessary degree from Dublin University are obscure. Swift is said to have been approached, and to have done nothing; but Swift was now on the verge of madness, and it seems unlikely that he was applied to. The attempt failed, and Johnson had to return to journalism.

Some months later Pope sent a copy of *London* to a friend. The poem, he wrote, was "by one Johnson who put in for a Publick-School in Shropshire, but was disappointed. He has an infirmity of the convulsive kind, that attacks him sometimes, so as to make him a sad Spectacle. Mr. P. from the Merit of his Work, which was all the knowledge he had of him, endeavoured to serve him without his own application; and wrote to my L^d. gore, but he did not succeed."

After he had been writing for *The Gentleman's Magazine* for a year and a half, Johnson was commissioned by Cave to report the debates in both Houses of Parliament, a piece of work which, if he had been more careful of his interests, would have put an end to his money troubles. Parliament had recently passed a resolution forbidding its debates to be reported in the Press. To evade this resolution, Johnson turned Parliament into the Senate of Lilliput—the Lords became Hurgoes, the Commons Clinabs, Walpole was transformed into Walelop, Pulteney into Pulnub, Pitt into Ptit, and so on.

Johnson himself only visited the House of Commons once, his reports were seldom based on anything more substantial than the names of the speakers, and were often entirely fictitious. Beyond taking care that "the Whig dogs" didn't get the best of the argument, he had little interest in the work, which he dashed off more quickly than most men could have transcribed the finished result. Shutting himself up in a room assigned to him by Cave, he allowed no one to disturb him, except the compositor or Cave's boy, to whom he would throw the copy without looking up.

Johnson's reports, though owing to his lack of dramatic power not in the least like debates, were widely read for their force and eloquence, and in time accepted both at home and abroad as the authentic utterances of English statesmen. William Pitt's famous reply to Walpole's sneer at his youthfulness fell not from Pitt's lips, but from Johnson's pen: "The atrocious crime of being a young man, which the honourable gentleman has with such spirit and decency charged upon me, I shall neither attempt to palliate nor deny; but content myself with wishing that I may be one of those whose follies

cease with their youth, and not of those who continue ignorant in spite of age and experience."

The sale of the *Magazine,* while Johnson was composing
these speeches, went up from ten to fifteen thousand a month,
and Cave so far relaxed his tight-fistedness as to buy himself
an old coach and a pair of yet older horses. But early in 1743,
when Johnson had been reporting the debates for more than
three years, he suddenly threw up the job on learning that
his speeches were being accepted everywhere as genuine. "I
would not be an accessory to the propagation of falsehood,"
he told Boswell many years later.

There is no record what Cave said when Johnson refused
to go on with the debates. Johnson was by now too important
for a man as prudent as Cave to quarrel with, but from this
date his contributions to the *Magazine* grew rapidly fewer.
The diplomacy he had used to get work from Cave was never
exercised to secure a decent wage, far less to obtain a share
of the profits he was making for the *Magazine.* He was always
careless about money, from the worldly standpoint, and in
his resignation of his work as a Parliamentary reporter he
showed a contempt for his own interests to which it would
be difficult to find a parallel in the history of literature.

(2)

While he was reporting the debates in Parliament, Johnson was secure of food and shelter, though Cave was, in Johnson's words, "a penurious paymaster." At other times, before and after this period, he sometimes reached the lowest
stage of destitution. During his friendship with Richard
Savage, he told Sir John Hawkins, the two of them spent

many nights perambulating the squares of the West End, being unable to afford the few pennies for a night's cellar.
When he had any money, he knew how to get the best value
for it. An Irish painter, whom he met in Birmingham,
sketched out for him a program by which a man could live
with decency in London on thirty pounds a year: ten pounds
for clothing and linen, one and sixpence a week for a garret;
a breakfast of bread and milk for a penny; sixpence for dinner; no supper, and threepence daily in a coffee-house, where
a man could find shelter for some hours and congenial company. On reaching London, Johnson followed this program
fairly closely. His dinner at the Pine Apple, off the Strand,
cost him eightpence a day. The rest of the company paid a
shilling, but Johnson saved by drinking no wine, and was
better attended to than the others because he always tipped
the waiter a penny.

How he provided for his wife and stepdaughter during
these years is obscure. When he first brought Mrs. Johnson
to town, he left Lucy Porter with her relations in the country; and later on she lived with his mother at Lichfield. His
wife he seems to have kept with him, whenever it was possible to manage it. The reference in the *Annals* to the silver
cup his mother gave him—"The cup was one of the last pieces
which dear Tetty sold in our distress"—shows that they strug-
gled through some of his worst times together. The only
recorded separation before the Dictionary was begun occurred in 1739, when he went to Lichfield for some months,
while trying to secure the headmastership of Appleby School,
and left Mrs. Johnson in London. A letter he wrote towards
the close of this separation still survives. Mrs. Johnson, who
was now fifty-one, was confined to bed with a bad leg; and the

letter is full of concern, both for her pain and for her anxieties about their situation. "You have already," he writes, "suffered more than I can bear to reflect upon, and I hope more than either of us shall suffer again." He begs her to call in a well-known surgeon, and not to be frightened of the guinea it will cost her, for he has just received twenty pounds, and has good news about *Irene,* which he is confident will be taken shortly, and so at length reward him for his perplexities. He still, the letter continues, looks forward to many happy years from her tenderness and affection, which he hopes their misfortunes have not yet deprived him of; and he concludes: "Be assured, my dear Girl, that I have seen nobody in these rambles upon which I have been forced, that has not contributed to confirm my esteem and affection for thee, though that esteem and affection only contributed to increase my unhappiness when I reflected that the most amiable woman in the world was exposed by my means to miseries which I could not relieve."

When Johnson was tramping the streets all night, he had to find some shelter for his wife. At one time, Sir John Hawkins says, she was taken in by a friend near the Tower, an arrangement which Hawkins characteristically conjectures to have been necessitated by Johnson's indifference in the discharge of the domestic virtues, though to anyone less boorish than Sir John this arrangement would suggest that Johnson used what little money or influence he had to secure for his wife the shelter he could not always afford for himself.

His worst sufferings were probably between his resignation of his work as a Parliamentary reporter, early in 1743, and his commission in 1747 by a group of booksellers to edit the Dictionary. Early in 1744 he published his *Life of Savage* anonymously. It was praised in the highest terms by Ralph in Fielding's paper, *The Champion:* "A more engaging or more improving treatise, on all the excellencies and defects of human nature, is scarce to be found in our own, or, perhaps, any other language." Joshua Reynolds, then a young man and unacquainted with Johnson, came across it by chance, and beginning to read it with his arm resting on the mantelpiece, could not put it down before the end, when he found his arm completely benumbed. But the public remained indifferent, and Johnson as poor as before. One day, shortly after it appeared, a Mr. Harte, who was lunching with Mr. Cave, spoke of it very warmly. Meeting Cave a little later, Harte was told that his remarks had given great happiness to a man who had been listening to them. Harte was puzzled, for he and Cave had been lunching alone. "Don't you remember I sent a plate of victuals behind the screen," Cave replied, and explained that Johnson had gone behind the screen to eat his meal because he was too shabby to show himself to a stranger.

The friendship of Johnson with a man of Savage's unbalanced character and dissipated habits led both Boswell and Hawkins to surmise that Johnson was occasionally persuaded by his friend to relax his principles where women were concerned. This surmise conflicts both with our general knowledge of Johnson's character and with what we can infer about the nature of his relations with Savage. Strict though he was in his own conduct, Johnson's interest in men, and wide sympathies, to say nothing of his poverty, had soon acquainted him with all the types of humanity to be met with in the squalid and violent London to which his lack of money condemned him. Savage, who was a fellow-contributor to

The Gentleman's Magazine, attracted him not as a guide to low life, but as a man, considerably older than himself, whose abilities and history were both out of the common. He was the illegitimate son of the Countess of Macclesfield, and, according to his own story, was persecuted by his mother with a ferocity which redoubled in its energy when he was on trial for his life, and only just failed to bring him to the gallows. When he first discovered who his mother was, he tried to see her, but she refused to meet him, and he used to walk outside her house at night for hours at a time in the hope of catching a glimpse of her when she came to the window, or crossed her room with a candle in her hand. These vigils are mentioned by Johnson, and were no doubt among the many experiences Savage recounted as he and Johnson walked round the squares of the West End. Savage had met the chief writers of the previous age, and had often though intermittently been in good society, and Johnson could therefore learn from him many details both about Pope and Steele, and about that class which his own circumstances prevented him from studying at close quarters. Savage, on his side, admired Johnson's brains and strong principles. "Abilities really exalted above the common level," Johnson says of him, "or virtue refined from passion, or proof against corruption, could not easily find an abler judge, or a warmer advocate." Savage would quickly have dropped a man as shabby and uncouth as Johnson, had Johnson suggested joining forces to pursue the women of the town, an enterprise in any case not likely to suggest itself to persons unable to afford even the shelter of a cellar. The respect Savage felt for Johnson is shown also by the fact that, morbidly touchy though Savage was, they never quarrelled, remaining on good terms until

Savage's death in a Bristol prison, to which his inability to settle his debts conducted him, after he had exhausted the benevolence of a number of Bristol merchants.

In his portrait of Savage, Johnson's sense of reality and sympathy are equally balanced. Against the faults of Savage, his vanity, his fickleness, his incapacity to learn from or even to admit his mistakes, his love of goodness unsupported by any sustained effort to practise it, Johnson sets his buoyancy under misfortune, his refusal to flatter the wealthy, and his right to be judged only by those who had been as persecuted by circumstances as himself. "Those are no proper judges of his conduct who have slumbered away their time on the down of plenty; nor will any wise man presume to say, 'Had I been in Savage's condition, I should have lived and written better than Savage.' "

Towards the close of 1746, Gilbert Walmsley wrote to Garrick: "When you see Mr. Johnson, pray give him my compliments, and tell him I esteem him as a great genius— quite lost both to himself and to the world." It was now nearly three years since Johnson had published his *Life of Savage,* he was no longer contributing to *The Gentleman's Magazine,* and an attempt in 1745 to raise subscriptions for a new edition of Shakespeare had failed. To his advertisement of this edition he had attached a criticism of *Macbeth* which Warburton praised as written by a man of parts and genius. But Warburton himself was bringing Shakespeare out, and his great reputation diverted the attention of the public from Johnson's proposed edition. Balked in this attempt to lift himself by some great undertaking out of the wretched life of a hack writer, Johnson nerved himself to a far more arduous enterprise, which he had long been turning over in his mind, and in 1747 published his plan for a Dictionary of the English language.

Great works, Johnson says in *Rasselas,* are performed not by strength but by perseverance. With strength he was endowed beyond most men; all his writings were composed with an energy and speed hardly matched in literature; but steady application was almost impossible to him. That he should have undertaken and carried through a work requiring such minute and sustained attention as a dictionary of a language which at that date possessed no dictionary of any merit, is an extraordinary proof both of the depth of the misery from which he desired to escape, and of his determination to escape from it. The idea of an authoritative dictionary had been discussed by Pope, who drew up a list of writers to be referred to, from the age of Elizabeth onwards. It is possible that Pope named Johnson as a suitable man for the task. "Were he alive," Johnson wrote in the plan, "he would not be displeased that I have undertaken it." But when Robert Dodsley, the head of the group of booksellers who employed Johnson on the Dictionary, first suggested it to Johnson, he said abruptly, after a momentary gleam of enthusiasm: "I believe I shall not undertake it." It was his poverty which at last drove him to the task. To compile a dictionary, he says in the plan, requires no higher qualities than that of bearing burdens with dull patience, and beating the track of the alphabet with sluggish resolution. But, he continues, though not a splendid employment, it was a useful one. Though it could not make his life envied, it would keep it innocent; it would awaken no passion, engage him in no quarrels, and expose him to no temptation from flattery.

With part of his nature Johnson desired glory and loved flattery, but his dread of the corruptions of the world was even stronger, and helped to reconcile him to the Dictionary. It is true that in his preface to the Dictionary written when it was completed, he speaks as if he had approached his task with the enthusiasm of a poet, not with the resignation of a drudge. He was resolved, he says, to enter and ransack the obscure recesses of northern learning, to display in triumph to mankind the treasures he unearthed, and to go behind words to things, piercing deep into every substance of which he inserted the name; but these, he adds, were the dreams of a poet doomed at last to wake a lexicographer. The enthusiasm here portrayed seems to be much exaggerated, in order to throw into stronger relief the grim reality which it preluded. It must have been with a gloomy eye that Johnson in 1747 surveyed the jungle through which he and his six assistants were to hew their way.

At the suggestion of Dodsley, the plan of the Dictionary was addressed to Lord Chesterfield, whose support as a wealthy nobleman interested in letters would, it was hoped, both advertise the work and assist its editor. That Johnson was not unduly sanguine about the value of Chesterfield's patronage appears from his reference to it in the plan: "How far this unexpected distinction can be rated among the happy incidents of life, I am not yet able to determine." It was probably only from a sense of obligation to Dodsley that he forced himself to pay the visits to Chesterfield imposed on him as a recipient of patronage. Chesterfield, who expected as little pleasure from these visits as Johnson, contented himself with giving Johnson a present of ten pounds, and was either not at home when he called or brought the visit to a close as quickly as possible. A few experiences of this kind sufficed Johnson, and he resolved to waste no more time on Chesterfield.

The sum to be paid Johnson for the Dictionary was one thousand five hundred and seventy-five pounds. He received this sum in driblets during the seven years he was engaged on the work, and at the close the booksellers discovered that they had, by some inexplicable freak of chance, given him a hundred pounds more than they had contracted to. Even with this unintentional bonus, Johnson, who had to pay his assistants out of his own pocket, did not receive for his own use more than about a hundred and forty pounds a year during the seven years he was engaged on the Dictionary. He had therefore to keep up his occasional writing. Three letters of his to the bookseller John Newbery survive, all dating from the middle months of 1751, and each urgently requesting a loan of one or two guineas. Such were his difficulties at a time when he had half completed the greatest single-handed achievement in dictionary-making in European literature. None the less, with the beginning of the Dictionary his worst days were over. He was secured against complete destitution, and his ability had received a kind of official seal.

One sign of the partial lifting of the oppression which had weighed on his mind was his poem *The Vanity of Human Wishes,* seventy lines of which he wrote in one morning at Hampstead in a small house rented for his wife in 1748. " 'Tis a grand poem, and so *true! . . .*" Byron said of it. "The infinite variety of lives conduct but to death, and the infinity of wishes lead but to disappointment." Byron saw only disillusion in the poem. His melancholy was born of

satiety, Johnson's of renunciation, and while Byron speaks
on his own behalf, Johnson mourns for mankind, in phrases
which reveal the poetic power buried in his nature:

"Patience, sovereign o'er transmuted ill."

"But few there are whom hours like these await,
    Who set unclouded in the gulphs of Fate."

"Still raise for good the supplicating voice,
    But leave to Heaven the measure and the choice."

Shortly before writing *The Vanity of Human Wishes*
Johnson renewed his friendship with Garrick, with whom
he had been out of touch for some years, and Garrick asked
him to contribute the Prologue for the opening of the
Theatre-Royal, Drury Lane, in 1747. It was ten years since
they had come up to London together, and Garrick at thirty
was already the most famous actor of the day.

Johnson's Prologue was brilliantly successful, and is interesting in itself because it shows how, whenever his mind
was kindled, it recognized the supremacy of the imagination
in poetry, and the baleful effects of moralizing. After praising Shakespeare as the greatest of dramatists—"Each change
of many-coloured life he drew, Exhausted worlds, and then
imagined new"—he passed to the Restoration dramatists,
condemned their obscenity, and celebrated the return to virtue in Addison. But nature, he laments, was no longer to be
found on the stage—"Declamation roar'd whilst passion
slept," and he concludes the Prologue with the hope that
Garrick would restore the reign of nature and of sense.

In spite of this hope, he raised no objection when Garrick
produced *Irene* at Drury Lane in 1749, ten years after he had

written to his wife that he had hopes of its immediate acceptance. He was very difficult over the emendations which
Garrick advised in order to make the play more attractive.
"Sir," he roared to a friend who was trying to keep the peace
between them, "the fellow wants me to make Mahomet run
mad, that he may have an opportunity of tossing his hands
and kicking his heels." He yielded finally, and the emended
play, supported by expensive staging and costumes, and a
caste which included four star performers, ran for nine
nights without provoking a riot. When Johnson was asked
how he felt at its failure, he replied, "Like the Monument."
He might have added "or the Bank of England," for he
cleared altogether nearly three hundred pounds, and in his
first exultation bought himself a scarlet jacket with rich gold
lace, and a gold-laced hat. In these he used to visit the green
room, and talk with the actors and actresses, and forget his
melancholy for a time. But his enjoyment of these hours began to alarm him, and one day he said to Garrick: "I'll come
no more behind your scenes, David, for the silk stockings
and white bosoms of your actresses excite my amorous propensities."

(3)

Mrs. Johnson was now sixty years old. Most of the few
extant references to her after her marriage with Johnson
speak of her poor health. "Perpetual illness and perpetual
opium" is the description Levett gave of her to Mrs. Thrale.

As soon as Johnson's circumstances were somewhat easier,
he sent her up to Hampstead, where she could benefit by the
country air, and accommodated himself and his assistants on

the Dictionary in Gough Square, off Fleet Street. He probably went to Hampstead for the week-ends, for it was there
he composed *The Vanity of Human Wishes;* and sometimes
Mrs. Johnson would leave Hampstead for Gough Square.
"Your poor Mamma has come home, but very weak," Johnson wrote to Lucy Porter from Gough Square in 1749; "yet
I hope she will grow better, else she shall go into the country. She is now upstairs, and knows nothing of my writing."

A fretful woman, likely to criticize her husband for no
particular reason, is suggested in this concluding sentence.
Mrs. Desmoulins, who sometimes stayed with her at Hampstead, told Boswell that Mrs. Johnson was captious with her
husband and wasteful of his money. As Mrs. Desmoulins, to
whom he offered the shelter of his house in later years, herself demonstrated, Johnson was one of those men who are
bullied by those dependent on them. Mrs. Johnson's small
fortune having vanished in the school at Edial, and the sub-
sequent years of hardship and repeated disappointments being made still less endurable by increasing ill-health, it is
probable that Mrs. Desmoulins did not exaggerate her ill
temper. Whether it was controlled by much affection, it is
impossible to say. That she retained her interest in Johnson's
work and believed in his genius is shown by her remark
when he began *The Rambler:* "I thought very well of you
before; but I did not imagine that you could have written
anything equal to this."

Johnson started *The Rambler,* a periodical consisting of
essays chiefly from his own pen, in March 1750, and concluded it in March 1752, a fortnight before the death of his
wife. She died during the night, in his presence, and he at
once wrote to his friend, Dr. Taylor, to come to him. It was

three in the morning when the letter reached Dr. Taylor, who hurried along to Johnson, and found him completely broken down. After they had prayed together, Johnson became calmer, but the next morning he wrote to Taylor again: "Let me have your company and instruction. Do not live away from me. My distress is great. . . . Remember me in your prayers, for vain is the help of man."

In a prayer which he composed a few weeks later, there is a sentence which shows that as his wife lay dying her thoughts turned from her own sufferings, now nearly at an end, to comfort and strengthen him: "Forgive, O merciful Lord, all my sins, and enable me to begin and to perfect that reformation which I promised her, and to persevere in that resolution which she implored me to continue."

There are many references to Mrs. Johnson in his Journal during the remaining thirty-two years of his life. "Thought on Tetty, dear, poor Tetty, with my eyes full," is an entry he made twelve years after she died, and on the seventeenth anniversary of her death he wrote: "This is the day on which, in 1752, I was deprived of poor, dear Tetty . . . my grief for her departure is not abated; and I have less pleasure in any good that befalls me because she does not partake of it." Nearly ten years later, he writes that, whatever their faults and failings, they had loved each other; and shortly before his death he prays for her, and wonders if she has heard his prayer, and is praying for him.

While she lived, he had been protected against the morbid terrors which assailed him in solitude; and the desire to recompense her for her sufferings and to justify her confidence in him had been a constant spur to his lethargy. When she died, he once said, a whole system of hopes and designs and

expectations was swept away, and nothing left but bottom-
less vacuity. Partly because of his personal handicaps and
partly because of his depth of tenderness, he needed marriage more than the ordinary man. "To be happy at home,"
he wrote, "is the ultimate result of all ambition; the end to
which every enterprise and labour tends, and of which every
desire promotes the persecution." The strength of his regret
for her does not, however, in itself imply that she gave him
much happiness. His remarks on marriage have in general a
disillusioned note. The lack of sympathy between his father
and mother occasioned many of his generalizations on marriage. But he was probably thinking of Mrs. Johnson in his
remark that a close union between a childless couple is
almost impossible; and when he says in *The Rambler* that
every animal revenges his pain upon those who happen to
be near, without any nice examination of its cause, and uses
this analogy to account for domestic bickerings, one cannot but picture him in his room at Gough Square, writing
hastily for the printer, with some sharp word from his sick
wife still echoing uneasily in his mind. The best he is able
to say for marriage as it works itself out in practice is that it
is not commonly more unhappy than any other experience.
It cannot, he argues, be eminently miserable, since so many
persons when the death of their partners sets them free enter
into marriage again, though in another mood he explains
second marriages as the triumph of hope over experience.
Marriage, he wrote in *The Rambler,* should be considered
as the most solemn league of perpetual friendship; a state
from which every artifice and concealment are to be banished
for ever, and in which every act of dissimulation is a breach
of faith. But between this ideal conception of marriage and

the common practice of married persons, both his own experience and his observation of others taught him that a great gulf was fixed.

(4)

The Rambler, though it did not sell widely, helped more than any other single achievement of Johnson's to establish him as a great moral teacher. His aim, he says in the last of *The Rambler* papers, had been to make them exactly conformable to the precepts of Christianity, without any accommodation to the licentiousness and levity of the age. In this aim he was completely successful, at some expense to the interest and value of his essays. When some passionate emotion, or the warmth produced by a sustained effort, as in *Rasselas,* melted his didacticism, he wrote some of the greatest prose in our language, and a few of the noblest verses. But the essays in *The Rambler* were neither long enough nor inspired by strong enough feeling to rise above his strict resolve to be instructive. Yet though heavy reading, they contain a number of scattered observations on life which illustrate both the depth and range of Johnson's wisdom. There is a close resemblance between him and Schopenhauer in their general view of human nature, though Johnson is detached and tolerant, and Schopenhauer nervous and embittered. Johnson's remark on the deceptions lovers practise upon each other is exactly in Schopenhauer's vein: "The whole endeavour of both parties, during the time of courtship, is to hinder themselves from being known." Schopenhauer's complaint over the obstacles opposed to genius are stated with equal force by Johnson: "The first appearance of

excellence unites multitudes against it; unexpected opposition rises up on every side; the celebrated and the obscure
join in the confederacy. . . . The strength and the unanimity of this alliance is not easily conceived." And Schopenhauer's general conclusion about existence is summed up by
Johnson in one sentence: "The cure for the greatest part of
human miseries is not radical, but palliative."

But Johnson was not a misanthropic recluse, and is both
more varied and more subtle than Schopenhauer in his estimate of human motives. "The vanity of being known to be
trusted with a secret is generally one of the chief motives to
disclose it," recalls La Rochefoucauld. More profound and
complete is his saying that though friendship implies beneficence, yet it is endangered by any extraordinary kindness
shown by one friend to another. Still more characteristic of
Johnson is his exposure of the popular idea that authors are
vainer than other men. The literature of self-justification
produced in the last ten years by all the chief figures in the
Great War, whether statesmen, generals, or members of the
Secret Service, lends a special force to Johnson's remark that,
if writers were as well acquainted with other professions as
with their own, they would realize that the egotism of which
they accuse one another is common to all mankind.

The necessity to get on with the Dictionary made Johnson discontinue *The Rambler* early in 1752. He had hoped
to complete the Dictionary in three years, and told Dr.
Adams that if the forty members of the French Academy
could compile their Dictionary in forty years, three years
ought to suffice a single Englishman. A little over seven years
is the time it actually took him, and it was published in the

spring of 1755. When the messenger who carried the last sheet to Millar, the bookseller in charge of the printing, returned to Johnson, Johnson asked him what Millar had said.

"Sir," answered the messenger, "he said, 'Thank God I have done with him!'"

"I am glad," Johnson replied, "that he thanks God for anything."

A few months earlier the attention of Lord Chesterfield had been drawn to the fact that the Dictionary was nearing its close. Chesterfield was an able man, and his letters to his son are a brilliant manual on the conduct of life in a wealthy and exclusive society, such as existed in France and England during the eighteenth century. But as he was himself small and ugly, and therefore balked in his ambition to be a perfect specimen of a fine gentleman, his admiration of manner and deportment became excessive even for an aristocrat. "How low and unbecoming a thing laughter is," he wrote to his son. "I am sure that since I have had the full use of my reason nobody has ever heard me laugh." Having martyred himself to his ideal of good form, he offered up his son, too, an awkward, simple-minded person, who had no taste for high life, was frightened by his father's attempts to cultivate his self-assurance, made a secret marriage with a poor girl, and died before Chesterfield.

Thinking that a few compliments to Johnson, whom he had ignored for seven years, would secure him the dedication of the Dictionary, Chesterfield wrote two papers in praise of the forthcoming work in a magazine called *The World*. The compliments he paid Johnson had nothing sincere in them except their note of condescension. Judging by the various works of Mr. Johnson already published, he says, there is good reason to believe that he would bring the Dictionary as near to perfection as any man could do. The language being in a state of anarchy, the old Roman expedient of choosing a Dictator to introduce order must be adopted, and he gives his vote to Mr. Johnson to fill that great and arduous post, and will not only obey him, like an old Roman, as a Dictator, but like a modern Roman will implicitly believe in him as a Pope.

In addition to compliments of this kind, Chesterfield was facetious in the last style likely to conciliate Johnson. England in the middle of the eighteenth century was predominantly Puritan outside the upper classes. Half an hour given to "the various works of Mr. Johnson" would have shown Chesterfield that the editor of the Dictionary was a severe moralist. Yet, in order to recommend the Dictionary, he tells a story of "a fine gentleman and a fine lady" who muddled an assignation because of a badly spelt letter. Such an example, he is convinced, must determine the fair sex and their adherents to adopt and scrupulously conform to Mr. Johnson's rules of orthography.

Johnson took no notice of these papers. "I have sailed a long and painful voyage round the world of the English language," he said to Garrick, "and does he now send out two cock-boats to tow me into harbour?" Chesterfield made another effort, dispatching a friend, Sir Thomas Robinson, who was charged to assure Johnson of Chesterfield's future friendship and patronage, and who on his own inspiration expressed his regret that he was not sufficiently wealthy to settle five hundred a year on Johnson; to which Johnson replied: "Sir, if the first peer of the Realm were to make me such an offer, I would show him the way downstairs."

Shortly after Sir Thomas Robinson's visit, Johnson wrote his famous letter to Chesterfield:

"February 7, 1755.

"MY LORD,—I have been lately informed, by the proprietor of *The World,* that two papers, in which my Dictionary is recommended to the publick, were written by your Lordship. To be so distinguished, is an honour, which, being very little accustomed to favours from the great, I know not well how to receive, or in what terms to acknowledge.

"When, upon some slight encouragement, I first visited your Lordship, I was overpowered, like the rest of mankind, by the enchantment of your address; and could not forbear to wish that I might boast myself 'Le vainqueur du vainqueur de la terre';— that I might obtain that regard for which I saw the world contending; but I found my attendance so little encouraged, that neither pride nor modesty would suffer me to continue it. When I had once addressed your Lordship in publick I had exhausted all the art of pleasing which a retired and uncourtly scholar can possess. I had done all that I could; and no man is well pleased to have his all neglected, be it ever so little.

"Seven years, my Lord, have now passed since I waited in your outward rooms, or was repulsed from your door; during which time I have been pushing on my work through difficulties, of which it is useless to complain, and have brought it, at last, to the verge of publication, without one act of assistance, one word of encouragement, or one smile of favour. Such treatment I did not expect, for I never had a Patron before. . . .

"Is not a Patron, my Lord, one who looks with unconcern on a man struggling for life in the water, and, when he has reached ground, encumbers him with help? The notice which you have been pleased to take of my labours, had it been early, had been kind; but it has been delayed till I am indifferent, and cannot enjoy it; till I am solitary, and cannot impart it; till I am known, and do not want it. I hope it is no very cynical asperity not to confess obligations where no benefit has been received, or to be unwilling that the publick should consider me as owing that to a Patron, which Providence has enabled me to do for myself.

"Having carried on my work thus far with so little obligation to any favourer of learning, I shall not be disappointed though I should conclude it, if less be possible, with less; for I have been long wakened from that dream of hope, in which I once boasted myself with so much exultation, my Lord, Your Lordship's most humble, most obedient Servant,

SAM. JOHNSON."

Men in high positions are generally careful not to expose themselves to attack from men whose abilities have not yet raised them from obscurity. But Chesterfield, although his chief interest was the strategy of social intercourse, had become so obsessed with the problems of high life as to forget that any danger could threaten him when he descended into the ordinary world. In taking advantage of this imprudence, Johnson was avenging both his own humiliations and those which intellect in all ages has to suffer from the insolence of power. His letter has a universal interest, though like all writing which rises to an impersonal significance, it is rooted in intense personal experience, in a lifetime of poverty and ill-health, and an exceptionally hard struggle for recognition.

Another emotion behind the letter, of a less exalted order, was hurt vanity. Johnson admired the manners of good society, and praised his friend, Topham Beauclerk, for never betraying when he was about to make a good remark or showing any satisfaction after he had made it. How far Johnson recognized his own shortcomings from the standpoint of a Chesterfield, one cannot say. Once, at the Thrales', he stupefied the table by asserting that he was well-bred to a degree of needless scrupulosity, that no man was so cautious not to interrupt another, that no man thought it so necessary to appear attentive when others were speaking, no man so steadily refused preference to himself, or so willingly bestowed it on another. And yet, he roared, everyone except Dr. Barnard, the Provost of Eton, thought him rude.

That Chesterfield was as obtuse about Johnson's social graces as everyone else, except Dr. Barnard, appears from "When I had once addressed your Lordship in publick, I had exhausted all the art of pleasing which a retired and uncourtly scholar can possess." The polished restraint with which Johnson rebukes Chesterfield was therefore partly assumed to show Chesterfield that a retired and uncourtly scholar could beat him at his own game.

Johnson's letter was the talk of the town, but though Chesterfield was in poor health, suffering from continual noises and pains in the head, he took the blow with great self-possession. Robert Dodsley, the publisher of the Dictionary, who was not interested in Johnson's private feelings, and had expected much benefit from Chesterfield's patronage, called on Chesterfield in an anxious frame of mind, and gave an account of his reception to Dr. Adams, whose Christian mildness had been shocked by Johnson's attack. The letter, Dodsley told Dr. Adams, was lying on a table for anyone who chose to read.

"I should have imagined," Dr. Adams said, "that Lord Chesterfield would have concealed it."

"Poh!" retorted Dodsley. "Do you think a letter from Johnson would hurt Lord Chesterfield? Not at all, Sir! . . . He read it to me; said, 'this man has great powers,' pointed out the severest passages, and observed how well they were expressed."

"Glossy duplicity," is Boswell's phrase for Chesterfield's adroitness, which exemplified his advice to his son never to reply to an attack in the same tone. But he was too much mortified to pass the matter off without some attempt to defend himself, and assured Dodsley that he had lost touch with Johnson through ignorance of his address, and that he would have dismissed his best servant, had he made any difficulty about admitting a man who would have always been more than welcome.

CHAPTER THREE

Domestic and Other Companions

(1)

IN the Preface to the Dictionary, Johnson expressed still more strongly than in his letter to Chesterfield the melancholy which overwhelmed him as he approached the end of his work. What praise the Dictionary will receive, he says, can avail him nothing in his gloom of solitude. Most of those whom he had wished to please had sunk into the grave, and success and miscarriage were empty sounds. "I therefore dismiss it with frigid tranquillity, having little to fear or hope from censure or from praise."

He was now forty-six, and could look back upon hardly any happiness, and upon only a fragmentary achievement as a writer. The common notion that he was indifferent to literary fame is based on his remark that no man ever wrote except for money. In talk he was sometimes cynical, partly to relax his moral muscles, and partly to conceal ambitions or desires which troubled him. His attitude to literary fame, as to many other things, is to be found in his written word, not in his spoken. A nation's authors, he says in the Preface to the Dictionary, are its chief glory, and he continues: "Whether I shall add anything by my own writings to the reputation of English literature must be left to time." His care for his fame is shown also by his revisions of his writings. There are many alterations in the second edition of *Rasselas*, he corrected his poems with care, and made no less than six thousand emendations in the second and third editions of *The Rambler*. Nor was the tranquillity with which he dismissed his Dictionary, though he looked upon it as a vexatious interruption of his real work, as frigid as he imagined. To the musician Charles Burney, at that time young and unknown, Johnson wrote very gratefully about his praise of the Dictionary. "Your praise was welcome," he said, "not only because I believe it was sincere, but because praise has been very scarce," and he added that among all his acquaintances there were only two who had not tried to depress him with threats of censure from the public, or with objections learned from those who had learned them from his own Preface.

Another reason for his melancholy was his continued poverty. In the year after the Dictionary appeared, he was arrested for debt, and had to write to Samuel Richardson for a loan of five pounds eighteen shillings to release him from the spunging-house.

But the chief source of his distress was his religious melancholia, which had deepened in the solitude left by his wife's death. There are two lines in *The Vanity of Human Wishes* which help to make clear the nature of his melancholia.

> "Where then shall hope and fear their objects find?
> Shall dull suspense corrupt the stagnant mind?"

He was, these lines show, frightened and sceptical at the same time. He knew neither what to hope nor what to fear from the unknown power which, vague though it was to his mind, filled his imagination with dreadful visions, in which he saw himself "suspended over the abyss of eternal perdition only by the thread of life, which must soon part by its own weakness, and which the wing of every minute may divide." These terrors were a symptom of the disease with which his imagination was infected. Had his imagination developed normally, his head would not have been bowed in panic before an angry God, but raised in confidence to the source of strength and joy which the untrammelled imagination divines beyond the material universe. "If our heart condemn us not, then have we confidence toward God." Exhausted by his sense of guilt, he abandoned himself to a morbid inertia, from which his sense of guilt would try to raise him, and exhaust him still further. In this vicious circle most of his life was spent. He was bound to what he was attempting to escape. His desire to use his gifts consumed itself in despair that he was neglecting to use them. How the energy which ought to have been employed in writing was drained away in making resolves, and reproaching himself for not fulfilling them, is shown in the following extracts from his prayers and meditations in the last thirty years of his life:

"Almighty God, forgive me that I have misspent the time past, enable me from this instant to amend my life."   (1757)

"My purpose is—To avoid Idleness. To regulate my sleep as to length and choice of hours. To set down every day what shall be done the day following. To keep a Journal. To worship God more diligently. To go to church every Sunday. To study the Scriptures. To read a certain portion every week."   (1761)

"My purpose is from this time—To reject or expel sensual images, and idle thoughts. To provide some useful amusement for leisure time. To avoid idleness. To rise early. To study a proper portion every day. To worship God diligently. To read the Scriptures. To let no week pass without reading some part. I will renew my resolutions made at Tetty's death."   (1764)

"I have now begun the sixtieth year of my life. How the last year has past I am unwilling to terrify myself with thinking."

(1768)

"The other day, looking over old papers, I perceived a resolution to rise early always occurring. I think I was ashamed, or grieved, to find how long and how often I had resolved, what yet except for about one half-year I have never done. . . . Whether I have not lived resolving till the possibility of performance is past, I know not. God help me. I will yet try."   (1773)

"Many years are already gone, irrevocably past, in useless misery; that what remains may be better spent, grant O God."

(1781)

This partial paralysis of his creative faculties did not affect his practical beneficence and love for others. His affections, which were repressed in his youth, were strong in his forties, by which age most men have ceased to care much for anyone except themselves. It was to conceal his intensity of feeling that he assumed the air of indifference which deceived Mrs. Thrale, who records that, though Johnson possessed the strongest compassion for poverty or illness, he did not even pretend to feel for those who lamented the loss of a child, a parent, or a friend. These were troubles, he told her, which those who lack food and raiment have no leisure to indulge. Like everyone who has been poor, it pleased Johnson to inform his rich friends that poverty was the only real ill. Yet when anyone he cared for died, he was overwhelmed at the time, and his distress perpetually renewed itself in later life. Many years after the death of Bathurst, one of his greatest friends in his early period in London, Johnson burst into tears when he was speaking of him to Mrs. Thrale. "My dear, dear Bathurst," he cried, "whom I loved better than ever I loved any human creature; but poor Bathurst is dead!" After Thrale's death, he used to sit with Fanny Burney "in long and melancholy discourses about our dear deceased master, whom indeed he regrets incessantly." When his mother's old servant, Catherine Chambers, was dying, he visited her and prayed by her bed. "She held up her poor hands," he wrote in his Journal, "and prayed with great fervour, while I prayed, kneeling by her. . . . She told me, that to part was the greatest pain that she had ever felt, and she hoped that we should meet again in a better place. I expressed, with swelled eyes and great emotion of tenderness, the same hopes. We kissed and parted. I humbly hope to meet again, and to part no more."

During his wife's life, she was the chief object of his tenderness. When she died, he had to find other outlets for his affection. Without her, he wrote to his friend Thomas Warton, he seemed to himself broken off from mankind, a solitary wanderer in the wild of life, a gloomy gazer on a world to which he had little relation. As the end of the Dictionary drew near, he may sometimes have pleased himself with the idea of marrying again. What would he find upon the coast, he wrote to Warton, when he landed after his long voyage? "A Calypso that will court?" The playful classical allusion probably concealed a desire which he was half ashamed of; and as he felt himself for many reasons debarred from realizing it, he resigned himself to lesser alleviations of his loneliness. The chief of these was the companionship of Miss Anna Williams and Robert Levett, the principal members of his famous household, which did not reach its full strength till the arrival of Miss Carmichael in the late seventies.

Macaulay's eloquent condensation of a number of scattered remarks in Boswell has given currency to the belief that the inmates of Johnson's household were, until rescued by Johnson, uncertainly poised between the workhouse and the lunatic asylum. This is much exaggerated. Although Johnson had, as Sir John Hawkins puts it, "a natural imbecility about him, arising from humanity and pity to the sufferings of others, that was prejudicial to his interests," he chose his household companions from other motives as well as from benevolence.

Though he had many friends, he needed closer ties. A man without children, he once said, stands forlorn and silent, neglected or insulted, in the midst of multitudes, and can find no one to whom his life or death are of importance, unless he has endeared himself to someone whose interest and gratitude may unite them to him. Miss Williams and Levett supplied in some degree the absence of wife and children. "The amusements and consolations of languor and depression," Johnson wrote to Mrs. Thrale, shortly before the rupture of their friendship, "are conferred by familiar and domestic companions. . . . Such society I had with Levett and Williams; such I had where—I am never likely to have it more."

Anna Williams, the daughter of a Welsh physician, came to London before Mrs. Johnson's death, and used to visit the Johnsons. Having lost her sight through an unsuccessful operation, she was taken into his house by Johnson, and lived with him, whenever he had a house, for the rest of her life, a period of about thirty years. Her temper was uncertain. Miss Laetitia Hawkins, Sir John's daughter, praises her kindness, while admitting that she may have been irritable with social inferiors like Levett; and others were impressed by her modesty, her courage under her misfortune, and the sweetness of her voice. Johnson, however, lamented her lack of good humour, and records that in her later years age, sickness, and pride made her so peevish that he had to bribe her maid with an additional half a crown a week to remain with her. But for many years she managed his house for him, regulating expenses, and furnishing the rooms properly, with stout old-fashioned mahogany chairs and tables. She was a good talker too; her acquisitions, Johnson said, were many, and her curiosity universal. In 1766 she published a volume of Miscellanies, which gave Boswell an occasion for the exercise of his detective faculties. Pressed by him to state whether he was correct in supposing that one of the poems in the volume was Johnson's, she replied sharply that the poem was written before she had the honour of Dr. Johnson's acquaintance. At the first opportunity Boswell laid his doubts before Johnson, who replied, "It is true, Sir, that she wrote it before she was acquainted with me; but she has not told you that I wrote it all over again, except two lines."

Miss Williams had the position of a wife in Johnson's household. To be taken to tea with her was a privilege bestowed only on his intimates. "I go to Miss Williams," Goldsmith exclaimed to Boswell, shortly after Boswell's first meeting with Johnson; and as Goldsmith strutted away with the doctor, Boswell looked angrily after them: "I confess I then envied him this mighty privilege, of which he seemed so proud," Boswell writes; "but it was not long before I obtained the same mark of distinction."

What Miss Williams was like as a hostess may not at this distance of time seem a question of much intrinsic importance, but the different opinions expressed by her guests are interesting, because they show how observation of facts is always modified by the observer's temperament. Boswell, who was regarded with suspicion by Johnson's household, says that Miss Williams's way of eating could not but offend the delicacy of persons of nice sensations, and that she had an awkward habit, when pouring out tea for her guests, of inserting a finger to ascertain how full the cup was. Baretti, an irritable Italian, said that he hated to see the victuals pawed by poor Miss Williams, who would often carve, though stone-blind. Percy, a decorous Anglican bishop, affirmed that when Miss Williams made tea for Johnson and his friends, she conducted it with so much delicacy, by gently touching the outside of the cup to feel the heat, that it was rather a matter of admiration than of dislike to every attentive observer. And Boswell, in a later edition of the Life, withdrew his first opinion, possibly through his hatred of Baretti, and adopted the Percy standpoint, though without mentioning Percy, whom he disliked.

To provide Miss Williams with some outside distractions, Johnson used to take her out from time to time, and was once seen with her at a fashionable reception, guiding her about with the tenderness of a father. She would sometimes accompany him, too, when he went to tea with his friends. Her pleasure on these occasions may have been mixed with alarm, for Johnson had strange habits bred by superstitious fears. One day, when he was calling with her on Sir Joshua Reynolds, he suddenly twirled her about on the steps, released her hand as the door opened, and made a prodigious leap over the threshold, while Miss Williams stood outside, waiting uncertainly for someone to lead her in.

Robert Levett was a general practitioner, whom Johnson first met in 1746, and established as a permanent inmate of his house about 1760. Johnson's ailments had from an early date interested him in medicine, and he was therefore glad to have at hand someone who was, in however rudimentary a way, a physician, surgeon, and apothecary in one. In his youth Levett had been in France, where he served as a waiter in a coffee-house much frequented by surgeons. He confided to them his ambition to become a doctor, and they raised a subscription to set him free to study medicine. Returning to London he acquired a large practice among the poorest classes, many of whom could only pay him with gin and brandy. He often gave his services for nothing, and never enforced payment. Yet, though he did not complain when he received nothing, it hurt his pride to exercise his skill without a fee, even if the fee were only a drink he didn't want. So he was compelled from time to time to become drunk in order to preserve his self-respect. When he was nearly sixty, a prostitute whom he met in a small coal-shed in Fetter Lane persuaded him that she was a near relation of a wealthy man, who was keeping her out of a large fortune. She on her side received the impression that Levett was a physician with a lucrative practice. They married in this double delusion, and Levett was so much incensed on discovering the truth that when his wife was arrested for theft he was only with difficulty prevented from attending the Old Bailey to hear sentence of death pronounced. She was acquitted, but they did not live together again, and from this date Levett became a permanent inmate of Dr. Johnson's house. The whole episode was regarded by Johnson as a fitting penalty for Levett's vanity in supposing himself a likely object for a young woman of wealth and family to fall in love with. Apart from this escapade, which was doubtless entered upon after he had been more heavily feed than usual, Levett was a steady modest fellow, and devoted to Johnson. Every morning, when Johnson was in town, Levett would join him at his late breakfast, and sit with him throughout the dilatory meal. He was interested in everything, Johnson said, and therefore a ready talker. Yet no one except Johnson ever heard him talk, and it is possible that the breakfast duologue was more often a monologue than Johnson realized. The meal over, Levett went off to his work, and the two would not see each other again till midnight.

A strange couple they must have appeared over their dish of tea, Johnson in a huge loose coat, a small black wig climbing up one side of his massive head, and Levett with his swarthy furrowed face, looking, as someone said, like an alchemist whose complexion had been hurt by the fumes of the crucible, and whose clothes had suffered from the sparks of the furnace.

Miss Williams lived with Johnson for thirty years, and Levett for over twenty. He got much happiness from both, and one should therefore discriminate between them and Mrs. Desmoulins, her daughter, and Miss Polly Carmichael, whom he added to his household in Bolt Court round about 1777, only a few years before his death. The chief recommendation of these three was their poverty. If he did not assist them, he said, no one else would, and they must be lost for want. But Mrs. Desmoulins had the further claim on him that she was the daughter of his godfather Dr. Swinfen, and Poll Carmichael appealed to him at first not only by her poverty but by her intelligence, which turned out to be spurious. The newcomers were unpopular with the veterans, Miss Williams and Levett, and Johnson, when Miss Williams attacked Polly Carmichael, used to support Poll with cries of "At her again, Poll! Never flinch, Poll!" But his liking for her soon faded. "We could spare her very well from us," he said at Mrs. Thrale's, where the company was listening to his account of the household. "Poll is a stupid slut. I had some hopes of her at first; but when I talked to her tightly and closely, I could make nothing of her; she was wiggle-waggle, and I could never persuade her to be categorical."

The kitchen, he replied to Mrs. Thrale, had fallen into a state of anarchy since the additions to his household. Levett reported that it was not what it used to be. So far as it was managed at all, it was managed by Mrs. Desmoulins, but the roasting was not magnificent, for there was no jack in the house.

"No jack!" Mrs. Thrale exclaimed. "Why, how do they manage without?"

Johnson replied that the smaller joints were managed with a string, and the larger were done at a tavern. "I have some thoughts," he said, looking serious, "of buying a jack, because I think a jack is some credit to a house."

"Well, but you'll have a spit, too," said Mr. Thrale.

"No, Sir, no; that would be superfluous. If a jack is seen, a spit will be presumed."

Time did not reconcile the veterans and the newcomers, and the veterans only bore with one another because they hated the interlopers more. Johnson himself was treated with asperity by the four women, and if he did one of them a small kindness the other three made a grievance of it. Still, such a life was better than the terrors of solitude, and besides there was a strong natural desire for sovereignty in Johnson, which life had imperfectly gratified, so his unruly little kingdom must have pleased him better than none at all. He had, too, a faithful equerry in Francis Barber, his Negro servant. Francis was brought from Jamaica by Colonel Bathurst, the father of Johnson's great friend, out of affection for whose memory Johnson interested himself in the young Negro, and took him into his service a fortnight after Mrs. Johnson's death. Except for two short separations, and a period at school which cost Johnson much more than Miss Williams thought he had any right to spend on a Negro, Francis was with Johnson from 1752 till Johnson's death in 1784. Sir John Hawkins suggests that Francis had nothing to do, a suggestion based on the fact that Johnson did not require, or rather did not make use of, Francis as a valet. But there were other uses to which Francis could be put. Johnson's house in Gough Square, and later his house in Bolt Court, were large buildings with many rooms. In 1775 Johnson assigned Boswell a room in Bolt Court, to use when Johnson kept him talking till the small hours. "I found everything in excellent order," Boswell narrates, "and was attended by Francis with a most civil assiduity." This glimpse of Johnson's domestic arrangements suggests that in his later years he lived in greater comfort and neatness than is usually supposed. After 1777 Francis must have had his hands full. The room formerly assigned to Boswell was now, as he records with a hint of annoyance, occupied by Mrs. Desmoulins, Miss Desmoulins, and Poll Carmichael; and it is not to be supposed that if Francis tidied Miss Williams's room, he would have been allowed to neglect the dormitory occupied by these three ladies. Levett's room, which at the time of his death was shared by another man, was also no doubt in Francis's charge. Nor, in the catalogue of Francis Barber's occupations, must his white wife be forgotten. She was eminently pretty, Mrs. Thrale says, and gave her Othello cause for uneasiness. Once, on a morning after a servants' ball at the Thrales', Francis left the house in a rage, and Johnson and Mrs. Thrale taking carriage set off in pursuit. "What is the matter, child?" Johnson asked, when they caught up with him. "Art sick?" Mrs. Thrale, unembarrassed by masculine squeamishness, reminded Johnson that it was jealousy, not sickness. "You stupid blockhead!" Johnson roared at Francis. "What do they *do* to her, man? Do the footmen kiss her?" "No, Sir, no! kiss my *wife*, Sir! I hope not, Sir!" "Then go back directly and dance, you dog! And let's hear no more of such empty lamentations!"

In addition to the bipeds, the household included one or more cats, the only one of which known to us by name is Hodge. "I recollect him one day," Boswell writes, "scrambling up Dr. Johnson's breast, apparently with much satisfaction, while my friend, smiling and half whistling, rubbed down his back, and pulled him by the tail; and when I observed he was a fine cat, saying, 'Why yes, Sir; but I have had cats I like better than this'; and then as if perceiving Hodge to be out of countenance, adding, 'but he's a very fine cat, a very fine cat indeed.'" When Hodge was ill, and on an invalid diet of oysters, Johnson used to go for the oysters, fearing that Francis would resent being sent out for a cat, and might take it out of Hodge in private.

Johnson's kindness was not confined to his household. As he had no belief in Utopias, he expressed his sympathy for the poor not by thinking out new societies in which everyone would be adequately fed and clothed, but by giving money to those who needed it. The view that persons already destitute could be pauperized by charity was condemned by him as a piece of Whig claptrap; and when someone objected that alms to beggars were spent on gin and tobacco, Johnson exclaimed: "And why should they be denied such sweeteners of their existence? It is surely very savage to refuse them every possible avenue to pleasure, reckoned too coarse for our own acceptance. Life is a pill which none of us can bear to swallow without gilding; yet for the poor we delight in stripping it still barer, and are not ashamed to show even visible displeasure, if ever the bitter taste is taken from their mouths."

Many instances of his generosity have been recorded, how once when he was down to his last half-guinea he parted with it to a stranger who stopped him with a tale of distress, how he used to put pennies in the hands of children sleeping in the streets, and how the beggars in the neighbourhood would line up for donations when he came rolling into view on the way to his tavern. The most famous of these stories was narrated in an anonymous pamphlet, published after Johnson's death, and its truth was confirmed by Mrs. Desmoulins. Once, in his last years, he was going up Fleet Street at two in the morning when he heard cries of distress. Following the sound for some time, he came upon a woman who was lying half-naked on some straw. She told him that she had been turned out by her landlord. Johnson looked about for a coach, but the streets were empty at that hour, so he wrapped his coat round her, lifted her on to his back, and took her home. The next morning he was urged, no doubt by the unanimous voice of his establishment, not to keep her in the house, for she had confessed that she was suffering from a venereal disease, but he replied that he was determined to give her a chance of reformation. She stayed with him for thirteen weeks, recovered her health, and was set up as a milliner in the country on the proceeds of a subscription which he organized.

The poor hacks who worked with him on the Dictionary were assisted by him to the full extent of his power for the rest of their lives. Twenty years after the Dictionary was completed, he wrote to a friend on behalf of one of them, saying he had given what he could, and begged till he did not know where to beg again. That morning he had given four guineas, and if his friend could supply another three, it would clear the man from his present difficulty. This man may have been Peyton, who died the following year. He is described by Baretti, who seems to have passed through life in a towering rage, as "a fool and a drunkard. I never saw so nauseous a fellow." The death of Peyton moved Johnson to write to Mrs. Thrale from a depth of emotion, and with a grandeur of language, which perhaps owed something to the recollection of the vigils which he had passed by the bed of his own wife:

"Poor Peyton expired this morning. He probably during many years, for which he sat starving by the bed of a wife, not only useless but almost motionless, condemned by poverty to personal attendance, and by the necessity of such attendance chained down to poverty—he probably thought often how lightly he should tread the path of life without his burthen. Of this thought the admission was unavoidable, and the indulgence might be forgiven to frailty and distress. His wife died at last, and before she was buried he was seized by a fever, and is now going to the grave.

"Such miscarriages, when they happen to those on whom many eyes are fixed, fill histories and tragedies; and tears have been shed for the sufferings, and wonder excited by the fortitude of those who neither did nor suffered more than Peyton."

(2)

Although Johnson wrote to Mrs. Thrale that the amusements and consolations of languor and depression were conferred by familiar and domestic companions, he also affirmed that a tavern chair was the throne of human felicity; and perhaps if he could have found a tavern that never closed, and could have dispensed with sleep and surrounded himself with unsleeping companions, he would have passed the whole of his life in comfortable forgetfulness of Miss Anna Williams's universal curiosity and Levett's ready flow of talk. As soon as he entered the door of a tavern, he said, he found a courteous master, and servants obsequious to his call, care and solicitude fell from him, and he abandoned himself to discourse with those whom he most loved, and to the delights of dogmatizing and of being contradicted. This last delight was one which no one present when he was contradicted ever suspected him of feeling. His impatience of opposition, Sir John Hawkins says, was recognized even before he became famous, and deterred many persons who wished to enjoy his conversation from seeking his acquaintance. These fears were exaggerated. Johnson recognized the right of every man to express his own opinions, and as long as this right was exercised with economy, and the opinions expressed approximated roughly to his own, he was the most cheerful of companions.

For our first sight of him enthroned as the monarch of a tavern gathering we are indebted to Sir John Hawkins. In 1749 when Johnson's commission to edit the Dictionary, and his receipts from *Irene,* had raised him above complete penury, he founded a club in Ivy Lane, for the purpose of free discussion. There were ten members, including Johnson, his great friend Bathurst, and Hawkins himself, at that time unknighted. Most of the members were Whigs, with strong views about the Young Pretender, whose campaign was still fresh in everyone's mind; but these views were suppressed out of deference to Johnson's affection for the House of Stuart. One of the members, Dr. Edmund Barker, disbelieved in the Trinity, but was so mangled by Johnson in his attempts to realize the club's ideal of free discussion that he ceased to attend. Another member, Mr. Samuel Dyer, after a youth spent in preparation for the dissenting ministry, had lost his orthodox faith, and adopted a mild humanitarian creed, one of the articles of which was that natural appetites required gratification. Dyer was very shy, and seldom spoke, and as he continued to visit the club, one may be certain that when he did speak it was not about the gratification of natural appetites.

It was difference of opinion which roused Johnson's violence, not difference of temperament. The strong sceptical element in his intelligence made him, by a natural instinct, savage in defence of his moral and religious dogmas; but towards persons, however unattractive, who did not threaten his peace of mind, his sympathy flowed out unchecked by his recognition of their defects. Hawkins, for example, was a man whom perhaps no one except Johnson ever treated as a friend, but as Hawkins's principles were strict, Johnson remained on affectionate terms with him for nearly forty years. "Why, really I believe him to be an honest man at the bottom," Johnson once said, adding in a meditative tone that to be sure he was penurious and mean and, it must be owned, had a degree of brutality and a tendency to savageness not easily to be defended. Hawkins, on his side, almost loved Johnson. In his account of one of the Ivy Lane suppers, there is a gleam of something like gusto as he looks back across forty years and sees Johnson's face "shining with meridian splendour, though his drink had been only lemonade." The supper, he narrates, was elegant. By Johnson's orders a magnificent apple-pie was served, stuck with bay leaves in honour of Mrs. Lennox, the guest of the evening, whom Johnson, after performing some ceremonies of his own invention, crowned with a wreath of laurel. It was at five in the morning that Hawkins observed the meridian splendour of Johnson's countenance. His own mirth had been abated by a severe fit of the toothache, which Bathurst vainly tried to alleviate by every device known to medicine. Gladly would he have taken his leave, but it was not till eight that he could withdraw, for the waiters were all in bed, and the delay in procuring the bill was a long one. Even without the toothache, and with the prospect of a good night's rest before him, the settlement of a bill was a painful experience to Hawkins; so one can understand his complicated misery as he left the tavern. He was ashamed, he says, at the resemblance the night's entertainment had borne to a debauch. Yet in spite of all this.

Johnson's joviality comes through to us in Hawkins's narrative, as Falstaff's would have, had it been reported by Malvolio.

Another club frequented by Johnson in this period of his life met in a poor alehouse in Ironmonger Row. There is no record of its meetings, which are reputed to have been passed by Johnson in reverential attention to an extraordinary person called George Psalmanazar.

Psalmanazar, who was nearly thirty years older than Johnson, came from the south of France. In his youth he had wandered about Europe, masquerading in turn as an Irish pilgrim, a Japanese convert, and a native of Formosa, an island off the coast of China. Arriving in England in his early twenties he composed a bogus history of Formosa with the assistance of a Scotch army chaplain. Although he moved Formosa to the coast of Japan, and credited the inhabitants with an interest in Greek literature, the book was accepted as a reliable history and sold widely; and Psalmanazar himself, as a Formosan convert to the Church of England, received donations from the pious, on which he lived at ease for many years. His penitence for this deception matured slowly, growing as the donations dwindled. It seems to have been fairly complete by the time he was forty, and the remainder of his long life was passed in the greatest poverty as a literary hack.

The respect and reverence which he inspired in Johnson were unqualified. Johnson said that Psalmanazar was the man he sought after the most in his life, and the best man he ever knew; that he would as soon have thought of contradicting a bishop as Psalmanazar, and that even the lives of the saints contained no examples of piety, penitence, and virtue superior to his.

There is nothing in Psalmanazar's *Memoirs,* which are written without depth or feeling, to explain Johnson's reverence for him. Where religion was concerned, Johnson suppressed his critical faculties. Reynolds said of him that though he was not easily imposed upon by professions of honesty and candour, he appeared to have little suspicion of hypocrisy in religion. Dr. Birkbeck Hill, Johnson's great editor, after quoting this remark by Reynolds, suggests that Johnson overestimated the piety of the reformed Psalmanazar, and turned a blind eye on the vanity and insincerity which Dr. Birkbeck Hill believes to have marked Psalmanazar throughout life. Against this view must be set the tribute of Smollett, who, though strongly anti-religious, praised Psalmanazar as a man who drudged in the literary mill for half a century in all the simplicity and abstinence of an Asiatic. This tribute is the more convincing because it explains Johnson's unruffled relations with Psalmanazar. No amount of religion in a man of positive character could have suppressed an occasional explosion from Johnson. It must have been the mild resignation of Psalmanazar which charmed and tranquillized Johnson, who was always struggling with his own passionate overbearing temperament. One pictures Psalmanazar as a benign old man, seated over an unsweetened glass of lemonade in Ironmonger Row, a stream of blameless sentiments flowing from his lips, while Johnson gently puffed and blew; or perhaps, like Levett, Psalmanazar never spoke at all.

Reynolds's remark applies more justly to Johnson's attitude to Hawkins, or to the novelist Samuel Richardson, who was one of the few men Johnson went out of his way to become acquainted with. His praise of Richardson and his censure of Fielding illustrate the conflict between his instincts and his principles. The masterpieces of both these novelists appeared in the middle years of the eighteenth century; but while Richardson's mixture of sentimentality and piety appealed to four-fifths of the reading public, Fielding was read only on his merits as a writer, and was widely regarded as immoral. Sir John Hawkins, for example, denounced him as the inventor of that cant phrase "goodness of heart": his *Tom Jones,* Hawkins said, sapped morality by teaching that virtue based upon principles is imposture, and that generous qualities alone constitute true worth. Johnson was equally violent. When Hannah More praised *Tom Jones,* he roared, "I am shocked to hear you quote from so vicious a book. I am sorry to hear you have read it; a confession which no modest lady should ever make. I scarcely know a more corrupt work." But Richardson he praised as the greatest of all novelists, and commended him especially because he had taught the passions to move at the command of virtue.

The "good fellow" morality of Fielding exasperated Johnson, who had fought against sensual indulgence all his life and therefore resented Fielding's view of it as an amiable weakness in the otherwise virtuous. The sharp distinction which Fielding draws between the generous vices of the flesh and the ungenerous vices of the mind—envy, hypocrisy, and cruelty—is in fact artificial, and is no longer insisted on in his last novel, *Amelia,* a book which Johnson, in spite of his prejudice against Fielding, read through at a sitting. But Fielding is on the whole incomparably sounder than Richardson. In his union of a realistic mind and a large heart he is more like Johnson than any other writer of the century. Yet though

Johnson's early years in London were those in which Fielding was writing his masterpieces in circumstances hardly less
difficult than Johnson's, they never met. Johnson sought out
Richardson in his stuffy parlour when he might have been
talking to Fielding in a tavern, and was misled by the technical
virtue of Pamela into overlooking the prurience of her creator's mind. His penalty for forcing himself to appreciate
Richardson was the discomfort he could not prevent himself
from feeling in Richardson's society. Whenever he spoke of
him, he would lead off with a eulogy of his genius and virtue,
and then descend to reality, remarking on Richardson's dread
of discomfort, and eagerness for trivial pleasures, or on the
insatiable vanity which made him fence himself off from outside criticism with a bodyguard of adoring women, and over-
tip servants in order to secure respectful treatment. If Richardson had lived to meet Mrs. Thrale, Johnson once told her,
her praises would have added two or three years to his life.
"That fellow," Johnson exclaimed, "died merely from want
of change among his flatterers: he perished like a man obliged
to breathe the same air till it is exhausted."

(3)

The image of Johnson as a stout old man is so fixed in our
minds that it requires an effort to see him as less than sixty
years of age. Yet when he and his bride rode to church, he
was a lean youth of twenty-five; when he perambulated the
squares of the West End with Savage he was not much older
and probably still leaner; and when he waited in Chesterfield's anteroom he was not the ample though rugged ancient
of the well-known painting, but a man of thirty-eight, who
for ten years had worked hard and eaten little. Nor, in his

relations with other men during these years, with Cave and Richard Savage and Bathurst, with Richardson and Psalmanazar, was he the autocrat we are familiar with. At this date he was still Mr. Johnson, and it is only with the founding of the Ivy Lane Club in 1749, when he was forty, that Mr. Johnson begins to fade and Dr. Johnson to emerge. Technically he remained Mr. Johnson till 1765, when Dublin University, anticipating Oxford by ten years, gave him a doctorate; but spiritually he was transforming himself into the Dr. Johnson everyone knows round about 1749, and was firmly established in that character by 1752, when the last number of *The Rambler* appeared.

From this date many of his friends were also his disciples, and the younger men began to seek him out. Bennet Langton, a member of an old Lincolnshire family, came to London when he was still in his teens, before going up to Oxford, in order to seek an introduction to the author of *The Rambler*. Johnson took an immediate liking to the earnest youth, whom someone once described in his later years as a very tall, meagre, long-visaged man, much resembling a stork standing on one leg.

Langton did not relax his principles on going up to Oxford, though he became an intimate friend of Topham Beauclerk, a grandson of the first Duke of Albans, and a great-grandson of Charles II and Nell Gwynne. They were drawn to one another by a common love of literature, and by the gratification each felt on finding himself attractive to someone of so opposite a character from his own. Beauclerk was very like Chesterfield, and had the same desire to excel in all the accomplishments proper to an aristocrat, from love-making to a taste in letters.

Through Langton, Beauclerk met Johnson, who was delighted by his resemblance to Charles II. They became friends at once, and remained on affectionate terms till Beauclerk's death twenty years later. Johnson once said that Beauclerk's talents were those that he had envied more than those of anyone else that he had known. Beauclerk was allowed to treat him with greater freedom than he permitted to others, but the polished insolence which Beauclerk affected sometimes grated on Johnson. "You never open your mouth but with intention to give pain," he once said to Beauclerk; "and you have given me pain, not from the power of what you said, but from seeing your intention." The relations of the two are vividly shown in this remark. Johnson forced himself to put up with Beauclerk's worldly airs, as he had forced himself to put up with Richardson's affected piety. The opposite and complementary weaknesses in his nature are revealed in these two friendships.

Another and far more gifted young man attached himself to Johnson shortly after *The Rambler* ceased to appear. It was probably towards the close of 1752 that Joshua Reynolds, then at the beginning of his quick rise to fame, met Johnson for the first time at the house of two ladies of some position, the Miss Cotterells. A friend of the Miss Cotterells, to whom they were indebted for many kindnesses, had recently died, and they were speaking of their grief. "Yes," said Reynolds, "but you have the comfort of being relieved from a burthen of gratitude." Johnson was delighted with this remark, defended it against the protests of the two ladies, and went home to supper with Reynolds. Boswell calls the remark "lucky," but there was more skill than luck in an observation so nicely calculated to please Johnson.

One day, a little later, Reynolds, his sister, and Johnson

called together on the Miss Cotterells. As Johnson in his shabby coat was plunging upstairs behind the other two, the maid caught hold of his sleeve and cried out that he had come to rob the house. "What have I done?" roared Johnson. "What have I done?" The maid released his sleeve, and he continued upstairs growling to himself. His mutterings continued after he had taken a chair, and his exasperation was increased when the Duchess of Argyle arrived and the Miss Cotterells presented him in a hurried, perfunctory fashion. While the ladies talked, he sat in a gathering silence which he broke at last, turning to Reynolds and saying in the accents of a bricklayer addressing a roadmender: "I wonder which of us two could get most money by our trade in a week, if we worked as hard as we could?"

These unphilosophic explosions of Johnson have astonished those who do not appreciate the truth that a philosopher's weaknesses are the raw material of his wisdom. It was after much self-observation that Johnson wrote: "All envy is proportionate to desire; we are uneasy at the attainments of another, according as we think our own happiness would be advanced by the addition of that which he withholds from us; and therefore whatever depresses immoderate wishes will, at the same time, set the heart free from the corrosion of envy."

The story of Johnson's friendship with Garrick, in its perpetual oscillation between envy and affection, provides a long commentary on this text. Johnson was exasperated at Garrick's quick rise to fame, both because Garrick had been his pupil, and because he despised actors, and thought the attention paid to them ridiculous. While everyone of importance, from Lord Chatham and Lord Mansfield downwards, was making a fuss of Garrick, Johnson treated him as if he were still at his desk in the school at Edial. One can see the schoolboy abashed before his master in Johnson's sardonic account of how one evening he met Garrick coming off the stage in a woman's riding-hood. "I came full upon him," said Johnson, "and I believe he was not pleased." It was no doubt a happy day for Garrick when the charms of his actresses frightened Johnson out of the theatre. That Garrick did not give himself airs with Johnson, but tried hard to conciliate him, is suggested by his heroic efforts to turn *Irene* into a popular success. Yet it is possible that he sometimes let Johnson feel the difference in the respective rewards which they had received from the world, for a few years later Johnson attacked him savagely in *The Rambler,* under the name of Prospero, whom he described as "a man lately raised to wealth by a lucky project, and too much intoxicated by sudden elevation, or too little polished by thought and conversation, to enjoy his present fortune with elegance and decency." Prospero's "sudden shoot of success," Johnson writes, filled him with an honest and disinterested joy, but the insolent airs of the man at last quenched Johnson's pleasure in his good fortune. That this attack was meant for Garrick we know from Johnson's own statement that Garrick never forgave it; and there were numerous impromptu hits at Garrick, uttered by Johnson and reported to their victim, to keep the wound unhealed. "A showman," Johnson once called him, "a fellow who exhibits himself for a shilling!" and, on another occasion, "A fellow who claps a hump on his back, and a lump on his leg, and cries, 'I am Richard the Third!'" Boswell was a tireless messenger of these sallies. Once when Mrs. Thrale was praising a line of Garrick's, "I'd smile with the simple and feed with the poor," Johnson cut her short with, "Nay, my dear Lady, this will never do. Poor David!—Smile with the simple; what folly is that? And who would feed with the poor that can help it? No, no; Let me smile with the wise, and feed with the rich." Boswell, who was present, conveyed these sportive remarks to Garrick, and was much surprised to find his sensibility not a little irritated by them.

The evidence about Johnson's attitude towards the election of Garrick to the Literary Club is conflicting. Hawkins and Mrs. Thrale represent him as without any provocation brutally rejecting Garrick's right to belong to such a distinguished gathering. But the more probable version is that he was annoyed on hearing that Garrick had said of the Club to Reynolds: "I like it much, I think I shall be of you," and that he forgot his annoyance as soon as he had roared out, "He'll be of us! How does he know we'll *permit* him? The first Duke in England has no right to hold such language." He cannot, however, be defended for his treatment of Garrick when he applied to Garrick for his very valuable collection of Shakespeare quartos, which he needed for his edition of Shakespeare. Garrick answered that Johnson could make full use of them, and that a fire and every other convenience would be ready for him whenever he wished to examine the collection. This offended Johnson, and he revenged himself by writing in the preface to his Shakespeare: "I collated such copies as I could procure, and wished for more, but I have not found the collectors of these rarities very communicative." Garrick was much incensed by this hit, and as usual said that he would never forgive Johnson; but some years later, when Johnson asked him for a loan of his Petrarch, another rarity in books, he sent it round at once. Boswell was present when it arrived, and reported the manner of its reception to Garrick. Seizing hold of the precious volume, Johnson, after ejaculating two or three quotations from the classics, was overcome by some obscure emotion, and raising the volume above his head dashed it to the ground, where it lay forgotten while Johnson stood motionless for some minutes, lost in a train of thought.

Although Garrick used to mimic Johnson as Tetty's lover, or take off his provincial accent, calling out to the company as with uncouth gesticulations he squeezed a lemon into a punch-bowl, "Who's for poonch?" he longed to be approved by him, for he was very vain and could not bear this striking exception to the universal applause. He was always planning how to impress people favourably, and when he told a good story or scored off an antagonist he used to leave the room as soon as possible, in order not to impair the effect. The fun he made of Johnson's contempt, putting into his mouth such sentences as, "Davy has some convivial pleasantry about him, but 'tis a futile fellow," concealed a constant mortification, and he would often try to conciliate his gruff tormentor. Boswell gives a delightful picture of the two together, one evening after dinner: "Garrick played round him with a fond vivacity, taking hold of the breasts of his coat, and, looking up in his face with a lively archness, complimented him on the good health which he seemed then to enjoy; while the sage, shaking his head, beheld him with a gentle complacency."

Severely though he attacked Garrick, Johnson would not allow anyone else to. He looked on Garrick, Reynolds said, as his own property; and he therefore resented any aspersions on Garrick as strongly as he resented the liberty Garrick took in having a career and reputation of his own. When Boswell hinted at the airs Garrick put on, Johnson said that it was wonderful how little Garrick assumed, and that if he had had the same applause he would have had a couple of fellows with long poles walking before him, to knock down everybody that stood in the way. Garrick, he said on other occasions, was the cheerfullest man of his age; the first man in the world for sprightly conversation; he was generous, he was a strict liver in a profession which gave more opportunities for laxity than any other, and he had advanced the dignity of his profession.

Once, when a clergyman, called Stockdale, asked Johnson if he thought Garrick really deserved the prodigious fame that he had acquired, Johnson replied, "Sir, he deserves everything that he has acquired, for having seized the very soul of Shakespeare; for having embodied it in himself; and for having expanded its glory over the world." Stockdale repeated this to Garrick. "Oh, Stockdale!" Garrick cried, the tears coming into his eyes; "such praise from such a man! *This* atones for all that has passed."

At the funeral of Garrick in Westminster Abbey, Johnson stood weeping by his grave. The next day he wrote to his widow: "Doctor Johnson sends most respectful condolences to Mrs. Garrick, and wishes that any endeavour of his could enable her to support a loss which the whole world cannot repair." Later he asked Mrs. Garrick if she would like him to write her husband's life, but she declined the offer, so he had to content himself with the famous compliment which he inserted in his life of Edmund Smith: "That stroke of death, which has eclipsed the gaiety of nations, and" (here Davy's old master took the pen) "impoverished the public stock of harmless pleasure."

CHAPTER FOUR

Rasselas—The Pension—James Boswell

(1)

JOHNSON was not very much better off after the Dictionary than before. The Dictionary had made him famous, but his inability to work except spasmodically kept him poor.

Early in 1756 he announced an edition of Shakespeare, for which he began to collect subscriptions. The terms of the subscription were that for one guinea down and one on delivery subscribers should receive the edition by Christmas 1757. Johnson sent some copies of these terms to his mother, who was still in charge of the bookshop at Lichfield, and wrote at the same time to his old friend Edmund Hector, asking him to get some of these copies from Mrs. Johnson and circulate them among his Birmingham friends. He concluded the letter with the hope that Hector would not only canvass for subscriptions himself, but stir up others to canvass. "The activity of a few solicitors," said Johnson, "may produce great advantages to me." In the April of the following year, he wrote to thank Hector for the subscribers he had collected. The subscription was not going forward quite as well as he expected, he said; and at Christmas of the same year he repeated this complaint to Dr. Burney. As the edition was due to appear by this Christmas, and Johnson had hardly begun to work on it, the slump in subscribers is comprehensible. His prayers and meditations show how much he suffered from his morbid inertia, but to the world he seemed to be living in comfortable indifference to his obligations. "I have several times called on Johnson," a friend wrote to Dr. Percy in the summer of 1758, "to pay him part of your subscription. I say part, because he never thinks of working if he has a couple of guineas in his pocket; but if you notwithstanding order me, the whole shall be given him at once."

It was perhaps to supplement the dwindling subscriptions on Shakespeare that Johnson started a series of essays under the title of *The Idler* in the spring of 1758. Some months later his mother, who was ninety years of age, fell ill. It was nearly twenty years since he had seen her. Until the Dictionary was finished, he was too poor and too busy to leave London, except for one visit to Oxford in connexion with his work; and afterwards he kept on putting off the visit he nevertheless longed to make to his home and old friends. "I have been thinking every month of coming down to the country," he wrote to Hector in 1756, "but every month has brought its hindrances."

On hearing of his mother's illness from Lucy Porter, who was living with her, he wrote at once sending twelve guineas, six of which he had to borrow. It must have been lack of money which prevented him from going down to Lichfield, for his desire to see his mother was very strong, and he wrote to her each day. "Your weakness," he said in one letter, "afflicts me beyond what I am willing to communicate to you. I do not think you unfit to face death, but I know not how to bear the thought of losing you." To Lucy Porter, a week after the first news of his mother's illness had reached him, he wrote: "I will, if it be possible, come down to you. God grant I may yet find my dear mother breathing and sensible. Do not tell her lest I disappoint her. If I miss to write next post, I am on the road." He wrote at the same time to his mother: "Neither your character nor your condition make it fit for me to say much. You have been the best mother, and I believe the best woman in the world. I thank you for your indulgence to me, and beg forgiveness of all that I have done ill, and all that I have omitted to do well." Mrs. Johnson died before this letter reached her. In the night after he heard of her death, he dreamed of his brother Nathanael, whom he had treated so roughly when they were boys, and who had now been dead more than twenty years. "The dream of my brother I shall remember," he recorded in his Journal.

To pay for his mother's funeral, and settle a few small debts which she had left, Johnson wrote *Rasselas* in the evenings of a single week.

A letter of his to Lucy Porter, a fortnight after his mother's death, contains some touches which help us to see the shop at Lichfield, with its two surviving inmates, Catherine Chambers, Mrs. Johnson's elderly servant, and Lucy Porter, now in the early forties, precise and a little tart. Lucy had passed from youth to middle age in the shop, looking after Granny, as she called Mrs. Johnson, to whom she had perhaps been drawn at first by sharing her disapproval of Samuel's marriage with Mrs. Porter. Anna Seward has painted a portrait of Lucy which reveals beneath the foliage of her style the lineaments of an original character. "With a marked vulgarity of address and language, and but little intellectual cultivation, she had a certain shrewdness of understanding, and piquant humour, with the most perfect truth and integrity. By these good traits in her character, were the most respectable inhabitants of this place induced to bear, with kind smiles, her mulish obstinacy, and perverse contradictions." Admitted into the best company of Lichfield, Lucy would yet, Anna wonderingly relates, serve in the shop when Catherine was at the market, rather than let Granny stand behind the counter at the risk of catching a cold. "There Lucy took her place, standing behind the counter, nor thought it a disgrace to thank a poor person who purchased from her a penny battledore."

Johnson, we learn from Anna, extended to Lucy a compliant indulgence which he showed to no one else. "I have seen her scold him like a schoolboy, for soiling her floor with his shoes, for she was clean as a Dutchwoman in her house, and exactly neat in her person." This asperity of hers with Johnson can be inferred from the tone of the letter he wrote her a fortnight after his mother's death. It is clear that she had taken him to task for neglecting his mother's dying wish that they should correspond regularly, and in defence he pleads his heaviness of heart, and begs her not to think it needed his dear mother's desire to make him write to her: "Every heart must lean to somebody, and I have nobody but you." He assures her, too, that he has too much confidence in her to accept her suggestion that she should send him receipts for the bills he was supplying the money to settle. He hopes that she and Catherine will continue to live in the house, and that Catherine will look after the shop. There will be no need for him to make a stocktaking—no doubt another of Lucy's punctilious suggestions. "The little trade," he says, "may go silently forward. I fancy Kitty can do nothing better; and I shall not want to put her out of a house where she has lived so long, and with so much virtue." He concludes the letter with the hope that Lucy will be willing to come and stay with him as soon as he can support her in comfort.

Three weeks later he wrote to her again saying he had not expected the inventory of little things which she had sent him, and that he could have taken her word for a matter of much greater value. As Lucy had been negligent about writing, he returned her reproach against him, and expressed the hope that she would make it a rule to write to him at least once a week. Unfortunately in his next letter, some weeks later, he had to apologize once more for not writing, but tried to appease her by saying that he was shortly sending her a little story book. This was *Rasselas*, which reached Lucy in due course, and which, it seems, she was very slow to acknowledge.

Rasselas, owing to the speed and energy with which Johnson wrote it, exhibits all his powers except the flashes of wit and humour struck out of him in talk.

Rasselas, Prince of Abyssinia, his friends, and the incidents of his story are of very slight interest. Their chief function is to provide Johnson with a number of texts from which to develop his philosophy. But that he should have chosen a heathen country as the setting of his reflections is interesting. The theme of *Rasselas* is the inherent imperfection of life. That this imperfection implies a state of perfection elsewhere is suggested in *Rasselas*, but nowhere put forward as the certain truth which, as a Christian, Johnson held it to be. Johnson always avoided theology in his writings. By placing his story outside Christendom he was able to confine himself to those intuitions of an ultimate reality which are common to all profound thought about the universe, Christian or pagan. "Every beast that stays beside me," Rasselas meditates in a passage which reveals the mystical strain in Johnson, "has the same corporal necessities as myself: he is hungry and crops the grass; he is thirsty, and drinks the stream; his thirst and hunger are appeased; he is satisfied and sleeps; he rises again and is hungry; he is again fed and is at rest. I am hungry and thirsty like him, but when thirst and hunger cease, I am not at rest. I am, like him, pained with want, but am not, like him, satisfied with fulness. . . . Man surely has some latent sense for which this place affords no gratification; or he has some desire distinct from sense, which must be satisfied before he is happy."

With the philosophies which affirm either that man can eradicate the desire for happiness, or that he can satisfy it, Johnson deals in two chapters. In the first he exhibits a philosopher who preaches stoicism. The man in whom reason is master, the philosopher maintains, is no longer the slave of fear nor the fool of hope. The philosopher's daughter dies, and when Rasselas tries to console him with his own precepts, he cries, "What comfort can truth and reason afford me? Of what effect are they now, but to tell me that my daughter will not be restored?"

The other philosopher trusts to instinct, not reason. He is an urbane eighteenth-century version of D. H. Lawrence, an optimist of the school of Leibniz. Voltaire's *Candide,* which was written at the same time as *Rasselas,* is also an attack on Leibniz, whose comfortable view of the universe provided Pope with the philosophy of his *Essay on Man*—"Whatever is, is right." In spite of his admiration for Pope, Johnson attacked the *Essay on Man* for its "penury of knowledge and vulgarity of sentiment." Pope, he says, having exalted himself into the chair of wisdom, tells us much that every man knows, and much that he does not know himself.

Deviation from Nature, the Leibnizian philosopher in *Rasselas* affirms, is deviation from happiness: "To live according to Nature is to act always with due regard to the fitness arising from the relations and qualities of causes and effects; to concur with the great and unchangeable scheme of universal felicity; to co-operate with the general disposition and tendency of the present system of things." Rasselas realized that this was one of the sages whom he should understand less as he heard him longer. He therefore bowed and was silent; and the philosopher, supposing him satisfied, rose up and departed with the air of a man that had co-operated with the present system.

Against the false simplifications of these two philosophers, who reappear in different disguises in every age, Johnson opposes the complex symptoms of man's innate dissatisfaction with his present existence. The picture which he draws of life is discoloured by his own abnormal gloom, but he hints at this limitation himself: nothing, he says, is more common than to call our own condition the condition of life. Apart from this discoloration, his survey of life is balanced and detached. There is none of the exaggeration which weakens Swift's indictment of human nature.

Children and parents, Johnson says, fall out with one another, because hope and despondency cannot agree. Domestic discord is not inevitable, but it is not easily avoided, and as it is always more easy to do evil than good, the wisdom or virtue of one can very rarely make many happy, but the folly or vice of one makes many miserable. The emptiness and ennui of power impress him more than its cruelty. The Pyramids, he says, seemed to have been erected only in compliance with that hunger of imagination which preys incessantly on life, and must be always appeased by some employment. Great disasters are rare, and the majority of mankind know nothing of war, plague, and famine. Though human life is everywhere a state in which much is to be endured and little to be enjoyed, national calamities and scenes of expansive misery are found in books rather than in the world. A fairly tranquil life is possible to those who limit their expectations. "Nature sets her gifts on the right hand and on the left." We must choose which gifts we prefer. If we are too prudent to make a choice, we shall obtain nothing. If we snatch at both sides, we shall seize neither.

His calmness deserts him only when he deals with sensuality. Marriage, he says, has many pains, but celibacy has no pleasures. By celibacy he means the unmarried state, the male adherents to which he portrays with the excessive severity of a much-tempted ascetic. Yet there is enough truth in the picture to make a thoughtful bachelor uneasy. "They (unmarried men) dream away their time without friendship, without fondness, and are driven to rid themselves of the day, for which they have no use, by childish amusements or vicious delights. They act as beings under the constant sense of some known inferiority that fills their minds with rancour and their tongues with censure. They are peevish at home and malevolent abroad, and, as the outlaws of human nature, make it their business and their pleasure to disturb that society which debars them from its privileges."

Virtuous celibates, however, are not represented as much happier than vicious. A hermit confesses to Rasselas that the life of a solitary man is certain to be miserable, but not certain to be devout; and an astronomer and a sage appear to enforce similar truths. Both these characters are portraits of Johnson himself; the astronomer, of Johnson in his hours of melancholia verging on madness; the sage, of Johnson in his serene moments. "I am like a man habitually afraid of spectres," the astronomer says, "who is set at ease by a lamp, and wonders at the dread which harassed him in the dark; yet, if his lamp be extinguished, feels again the terrors which he knows that when it is light he shall feel no more." An analysis of Johnson's own melancholia follows. No disease of the imagination, he says, is so hard to cure as that which is complicated with the dread of guilt. Sensual images can be repelled, but images which take the form of moral obligations enslave the mind, which is afraid to drive them away.

The morbid strain in Johnson, which is here analysed, is revealed directly at the beginning of the book in a sentence which makes more vivid to us the terrors he suffered in solitude. He is describing the Happy Valley in which Rasselas passed his early years, and writes, almost in the style of Poe: "The lake discharged its superfluities by a stream which entered a dark cleft of the mountain on the northern side, and fell with dreadful noise from precipice to precipice, till it was heard no more."

The portrait of the sage is of Johnson in his sane daylight wisdom. Hardly anyone could paint himself as a wise and melancholy old man without falling into self-consciousness and sentimentality, but Johnson's portrait has no trace of either. "Praise is to an old man an empty sound. I have neither mother to be delighted with the reputation of her son, nor wife to partake the honours of her husband. I have outlived my friends and rivals. Nothing is now of much importance;

for I cannot extend my interest beyond myself. . . . Riches would now be useless, and high employment would be pain. My retrospect of life recalls to my view many opportunities of good neglected, much time squandered upon trifles, and more lost in idleness and vacancy. I leave many great designs unattempted, and many great attempts unfinished. My mind is burdened with no heavy crime, and therefore I compose myself to tranquillity; endeavour to abstract my thoughts from hopes and cares which, though reason knows them to be vain, still try to keep their old possession of the heart; expect, with serene humility, that hour which nature cannot long delay, and hope to possess in a better state that happiness which here I could not find, and that virtue which here I have not attained."

(2)

The absence of any gleam of happiness in *Rasselas,* though partly due to Johnson's innate melancholy, was also due to the poverty which had attended him throughout life. He had a capacity for enjoyment which did not need much money for its cultivation, but required more than his charity to others had ever spared for his own use.

With the balance of his proceeds from *Rasselas* he treated himself to his second excursion from London in twenty years, visiting Oxford in July 1759. Forgetting the farewell to the vanities of this world which he had spoken through the mouth of the sage in *Rasselas,* he wore his Master of Arts gown throughout his visit. "I have been in my gown ever since I came here," he recorded. "It was, at my first coming, quite new and handsome." He also took the dangerous swim which

Hawkins mentions, drank three bottles of port without losing command of his faculties, and, perhaps on the same occasion, challenged an elderly professor to climb over the wall of University College.

After this outburst he returned to London and the oppression of his uncompleted Shakespeare. His melancholy increased during the next two years. On Easter Eve, 1761, he wrote in his Journal: "Since the communion of last Easter I have led a life so dissipated and useless, and my terrours and perplexities have so much increased, that I am under great depression and discouragement." In the winter of this year he again left London, to revisit Lichfield after more than twenty years, but, as we learn from a letter to Baretti, the visit brought him no happiness. He found the streets much narrower than he had remembered them. A new race of people, who hardly knew him, had sprung up. His playfellows had grown old, and his stepdaughter had lost the beauty and gaiety of youth, without having gained much of the wisdom of age. "I wandered about for five days," he concludes, "and took the first convenient opportunity of returning to a place, where, if there is not much happiness, there is, at least, such a diversity of good and evil, that slight vexations do not fix upon the heart."

This letter to Baretti, which is a very long one, was written on July 20, 1762, the day on which Johnson's poverty was ended for ever by the bestowal of an annual pension of three hundred pounds. It is characteristic of his repressed nature that he does not tell Baretti of the pension. He was too doubtful about worldly happiness, and too much on his guard against life, to give way to exultation, or even to express his relief. It is only the length of the letter which shows that he was moved and needed an outlet for his emotions. To Lucy Porter, a few days later, he communicated the good news in a brief note: "If I write but seldom to you it is because it seldom happens that I have anything to tell you that can give you pleasure, but last Monday I was sent for by the Chief Minister, the Earl of Bute, who told me that the King had empowered him to do something for me; and let me know that a pension was granted me of three hundred a year. Be so kind as to tell Kitty."

Another reason for his reserve was the momentary uneasiness he felt at accepting a pension at all. In his Dictionary he had defined a pension as "an allowance made to anyone without an equivalent. In England it is generally understood to mean pay given to a state hireling for treason to his country." This definition was written in the reign of George II, whom Johnson disliked both as a man and as a usurper of a throne which ought to have been occupied by a Stuart. But Johnson's Jacobitism was not profound, and by 1762, when the new king, George III, had been on the throne two years, it was only a romantic memory. In the following year, referring to the numerous attacks on his pension, he said to Boswell: "It is true, that I cannot now curse" (smiling) "the House of Hanover; nor would it be decent for me to drink King James's health in the wine that King George gives me money to pay for. But, Sir, I think that the pleasure of cursing the House of Hanover, and drinking King James's health are amply overbalanced by three hundred pounds a year." His definitions of pension and pensioner were naturally the main weapons of his assailants, who continued to attack him over a number of years, without drawing from him anything but

the remark that he wished they would make twice the noise
if that would make his pension twice the size.

His definition of pensioner was more serious than his definition of pension, and gives a better clue to the uneasiness he
felt when the pension was first suggested to him. A pensioner,
he had written, was "One who is supported by an allowance
paid at the will of another; a dependant." He was reluctant
to place himself at anyone's mercy, and accepted the pension
only after he was satisfied that it was offered to him in recognition of his past work, not as a fee to support the Government
with his pen.

Johnson owed his pension largely to his dislike of the
Scots. The Prime Minister, Lord Bute, was a Scot, and Wedderburne, who pressed Johnson's claim on Bute, was one of
the Scottish politicians with whom Bute had surrounded himself, to the disgust of English place-hunters. There was a general feeling in London that the Scots were getting all the
prizes, and Wedderburne therefore thought it would be
judicious to confer a pension on Johnson, a great English
figure, who was known to be unfriendly to Scotland. Wedderburne was acquainted with Johnson, but he remembered the
fate of the bookseller, Tom Osborne; and not wishing to be
felled to the earth, should Johnson resent the offer, he asked
one of Johnson's friends, Arthur Murphy, to break it to him.
The offer, Murphy records, was conveyed by slow and studied
approaches. It threw Johnson into a profound meditation,
from which he emerged to ask Murphy for twenty-four hours
in which to think it over. At their next meeting he accepted
the offer, and on the following day was escorted by Wedderburne to the Prime Minister. "Pray, my Lord," he asked

Bute, "what am I expected to do for this pension?" Bute replied that he was expected to do nothing. This pleased Johnson on every ground. "It is not given you for anything you are to do, but for what you have done," Bute said, and twice repeated the assurance, in order to set Johnson's mind completely at ease.

Johnson was within a few weeks of his fifty-fourth birthday, when this brief and pleasant interview put an end to his struggle with external circumstances.

Less than four weeks after his audience with Bute, Johnson left London with Reynolds for a journey through Devonshire. At Plymouth, where he stayed for some weeks, he identified himself with the old town against the new one which was growing up round the dockyard, and the inhabitants of which were named dockers. "I *hate* a docker," he was heard to exclaim passionately; and when the dockers petitioned that some of the water which supplied Plymouth might be diverted to their use Johnson cried, "No, no! I am against the dockers; I am a Plymouth man. Rogues! Let them die of thirst. They shall not have a drop!" His exuberance also revealed itself at the table. At one house the enormous quantity of honey, cream, and cider which he consumed alarmed the host, who waited in anxious silence for some sign of distress, but the strength of Johnson's constitution saved him from any unpleasant consequences. At another house he drank three bottles of wine after dinner, found himself unable to articulate a difficult word, persevered till he was successful, and then, remarking to Reynolds that it was time to go to bed, left the room.

This was the first of many journeys. Travel, now that he

could afford it, was a distraction he valued less only than talk. Once, on the way to Derby, he said to Boswell, "If I had no duties, and no reference to futurity, I would spend my life in driving briskly in a post-chaise with a pretty woman; but she should be one who could understand me, and would add something to the conversation."

No year of the remaining twenty-two of his life passed without his leaving London on some expedition, which would occupy anything from a fortnight to six months. Cambridge and Beaconsfield, Salisbury, Rochester, and Harwich were among the places he visited; and he made almost annual pilgrimages to Lichfield, Oxford, and Ashbourne, near Derby, the home of his friend, Dr. Taylor. In addition to these lesser excursions, there were the journeys to North Wales and to Paris with the Thrales, and to the Hebrides with Boswell; and plans for still longer voyages. When he was nearly seventy, he tried to persuade Boswell to sail with him up the Baltic, but Boswell was evasive, saying that he wished to see Wales, and regretting that Johnson had already been there. "It is a pity he has not a better bottom," Johnson wrote to Mrs. Thrale of Boswell's faint-heartedness. He was also to have gone to Italy with the Thrales in the previous year; but their son died, and the journey was postponed and finally cancelled. "A man who has not been to Italy," said Johnson, "is always conscious of an inferiority. . . . The grand object of travelling is to see the shores of the Mediterranean." Poland, India, and even a voyage round the world were all contemplated by him. "If I had money enough, what would I do?" he once wrote to Mrs. Thrale. "Perhaps if you and master did not hold me, I might go to Cairo, and down the Red Sea to Bengal, and take a ramble to India."

Love of life and a boundless melancholy were always contending in him. "Is not mine a kind of life turned upside down?" he wrote to Taylor on his return from France. "Fixed to a spot when I was young, and roving the world when others are contriving to sit still, I am wholly unsettled." But his travels brought out a capacity for enjoyment buried in his earlier years. He often said to Boswell that their journey to the Hebrides was the best experience of his life, and once asked him if he would lose the recollection of it for five hundred pounds.

(3)

It was on May 16, 1763, that Johnson and James Boswell, now in his twenty-third year, met for the first time. Boswell's childhood and early youth had been passed on the family estate of Auchinleck, in Ayrshire, under the accusing eye of his father, Alexander Boswell, a judge in the Scottish Courts of Session. Although life on the family estate was uncomfortable to him while his father was alive, and tedious when he himself was the Laird, except for one brief period in the character of a firm but kindly feudal landlord, Boswell was proud of Auchinleck. The "sullen dignity" of the old castle, from which the family had moved to a modern mansion, made him even more conscious of his ancient lineage than at other times, and to ancient lineage he attached the highest value. In his sketch of Mr. Thrale, who was a brewer, he comments on the increasing tendency of the age to admit wealthy merchants into the ranks of the gentry. Does not the too rapid advance of men of low extraction, he wonders, tend to lessen the value of that distinction by birth and gentility, which has ever been found beneficial to the grand scheme of subordination? Are not the arguments in favour of rewarding the spirited hazards of trade and commerce with those flattering distinctions by which mankind are so universally captivated false, though specious? "To refute them is needless," he exclaims abruptly. "The general sense of mankind cries out, with irresistible force, 'un gentilhomme est toujours gentilhomme.' "

Alexander Boswell wished his son to be a lawyer, and James, after matriculating in moral philosophy and rhetoric at Glasgow University, went to Edinburgh to pursue his legal studies. Although he compared himself as a law student to a Newmarket courser tied to a dung-cart, he must have occasionally glanced at a law-book, for he was admitted as a Scotch advocate in 1766, and twenty years later, in a spasm of forensic zeal, was called to the English Bar. But his youthful ambitions ranged in other directions. He longed to be an officer in the Guards, because of the handsome uniform, which he hoped would recommend him to "ladies of quality, beauty, and fortune." The military aspect of an officer's career appealed to him less strongly, for he was physically timid except when listening to music, which produced in him, he says, alternate sensations of pathetic dejection, so that he was ready to shed tears, and of daring resolution, so that he was inclined to rush into the thickest part of the battle. He also longed to be a writer, and before his twenty-third year had published a good deal of verse, including an *Ode to Tragedy*, which he prefaced with a sketch of himself as "a most excellent man, of an ancient family in the west of Scotland, upon which he values himself not a little. He is somewhat of a humorist and a little tinctured with pride. He has a good manly countenance, and he owns himself to be amorous. He has infinite vivacity, yet is observed at times to have a melancholy cast. He is rather fat than lean, rather short than tall, rather young than old." A third ambition was to lead an orderly existence. His great object, he told a youthful friend, was to attain a proper conduct in life, and to restrain the dissipation and folly in which he was tempted to drown his natural melancholy. But to classify his ambitions is to give them a misleading air of evolving out of each other in a regular sequence. There were probably few days in his youth, or indeed in his life, when a panorama of all the Boswells who had paraded before his fancy in the preceding twenty-four hours would not have displayed Boswell the feudal lord, Boswell roaming foreign strands, Boswell the gay toper, Boswell brooding apart, Boswell the king of infidel wits, Boswell the pillar of orthodox piety, Boswell the loyal husband, Boswell seducing a Duchess, Boswell scattering plenty o'er a smiling land, Boswell wading through slaughter to a throne.

This appetite for every kind of experience was accompanied by an impersonal interest in the medley of human desires and ambitions. Boswell had in the highest degree the dramatic poet's enjoyment of the spectacle of existence. To watch the drama entranced him as much as to act in it. When in his letters he sometimes speaks of himself in the third person, he is actuated not only by vanity but also by a sudden perception of Boswell as an intriguing character, whom he has had unusual opportunities of studying at close quarters. Interested by Boswell as a man who governs his life on a predetermined plan, he writes: "Boswell when cool and sedate fixes rules for Boswell to live by in the common course of life, when perhaps Boswell might be dissipated and forget the distinctions between right and wrong, between propriety and impropriety." Conscious of Boswell as a rich nature, not to be for ever hampered by pedantic rules of conduct, he writes: "She was indeed a fine, strong, spirited girl, a whore worthy of Boswell, if Boswell must have a whore." But his power of detachment was as unstable as all his other qualities. From this lofty survey of Boswell matched with an opponent worthy of his steel, he drops in the next sentence to—"I am abashed, and determined to keep the strictest watch over my passions." This perpetual oscillation between one mood and another is Boswell's chief characteristic. Had he been able to unify his feelings and his thoughts, he would have been a great dramatic poet, but he had no centre around which to group his intellectual and emotional existence. Neither in his life nor in his writings could he exercise any control over his impressionability to the mood of the moment. As in his life he passed from woman to woman, and drinking bout to drinking bout, so in his biography of Johnson he passed from episode to episode, making each as vivid as the reality it portrayed, but unable to relate them to one another in an organic whole. The common view of him as foolish to the verge of imbecility derives from his lack of control. A reputation for wisdom is more easily gained by a man who has only one idea and sticks to it, than by a man with a thousand ideas which he is always chasing in different directions. In Boswell's criticism of *Rasselas,* for example, each point taken separately is sensible enough, but the criticism as a whole is completely incoherent. He begins by praising the truth and wisdom of *Rasselas* without any qualification. He then suggests that Johnson's morbid melancholy distorts his picture of existence. He then returns to his first standpoint. He then abandons it in favour of a maxim which he had heard from a Turkish lady educated in France: "Ma foi, Monsieur, notre bonheur dépend de la façon que notre sang circule." He then returns again to his first standpoint, enlarging on it with a plea to his readers to realize that this life is only a passage to a better, and that it is a part of the mysterious plan of Providence that intellectual beings must be made perfect through suffering. He then qualifies this depressing conclusion by urging that, if we walk with hope in the midday sun of revelation, we shall derive a considerable relish from the comforts and enjoyments of our pilgrimage. He then forgets all about the midday sun of revelation, and adopts Voltaire's view that in spite of everything the world is a passable place. From this he passes to a caution against thinking too deeply about anything, advocates the cultivation, under the command of good principles, of agreeable sensations, and rounds off with "Mr. Burke's admirable advice to a grave and anxious gentleman 'to live pleasant.' "

Being unable to impose any order on his jumble of desires, opinions, and ambitions, Boswell was attracted towards anyone whose firmness promised him some kind of support. His friendship with William Temple, a sedate clergyman, lasted throughout his life, and he made Temple the confidant of all his love affairs. In this candour there was, as usual, a confusion of motives. It pleased his vanity to emphasize the contrast between his own exciting experiences and his friend's life of humdrum virtue. "This is a curious letter to a clergyman," he says, after praising his mistress as admirably formed for amorous dalliance, while damning her for a lewd minx. At the same time he was envious of Temple's tranquil existence, and saw in his friendship with so virtuous man a kind of guarantee that he too would one day find a steady footing in life. "You may depend upon it," he wrote to Temple, after narrating how he had been unfaithful to his mistress with a prostitute, "that very soon my follies will be at an end, and I shall turn out an admirable member of society."

This desire to find in someone else the centre he could not find in himself was one of the chief incentives to his pursuit of well-known men. When he was only eighteen, he sought out David Hume, then at the height of his fame. "A very proper person for a young man to cultivate an acquaintance with," he wrote to Temple, "though he has not perhaps the most delicate taste." But Hume was too mild and detached either to sustain him morally or to satisfy his other two objects in seeking out remarkable men, the gratification of his vanity, and the pleasure of watching human nature in its most interesting embodiments.

After Hume came Sterne, whom Boswell met on his first visit to London. But Sterne did not attract Boswell. Wit and genius, unsupported by force of character, never stirred more than a momentary enthusiasm in him. He despised Goldsmith for his shiftlessness, and Sterne no doubt repelled him by his volatility. What he desired was friendship with men whom he could esteem, men whose appreciation of his merits would stimulate his self-respect and his self-confidence, both of which his father's contempt had stunted throughout his early years. The men he attached or tried to attach himself to, Johnson, Paoli, Chatham, Voltaire, Rousseau, and Wilkes, all possessed either the seriousness of purpose or the daring which he felt to be lacking in himself.

The attraction which Johnson exercised over Boswell,

even before they met, was already powerful. Moral support, the gratification of his vanity, and food for his interest in human nature, were all to be found in a friendship with Johnson, the chief moralist of the age, its greatest literary figure, and its most extraordinary character. Johnson's fascination as a character was perhaps hardly guessed at by Boswell before they met, but the other two incentives to make his acquaintance arose out of the nature and extent of Johnson's reputation, now almost at its full height. Beneath his bluster, Boswell, at any rate in his youth, had enough diffidence to prevent him from looking forward to a close connexion with Johnson. All he hoped for was an occasional meeting to provide material for a letter to his friend Temple. This hope was disappointed during his first visit to London by the failure of a friend to fulfil his promise of arranging a meeting between Boswell and Johnson. The inaccessibility of the great man awed and at the same time stimulated Boswell.

When he was next in London, three years later, he made friends with Thomas Davies, an ex-actor and bookseller, whom Johnson used often to visit, and whom Boswell therefore called on again and again, until at last his pertinacity was rewarded. One afternoon when he was taking tea with Davies in the back shop, Davies perceived Johnson through the glass door between the back and front shop, and turning to Boswell announced his approach in the manner of Horatio warning Hamlet that his father's ghost is drawing near.

The mixture of guile and candour which marked all Boswell's relations with Johnson is perfectly illustrated by his disingenuous account of how he provoked the first remark which Johnson addressed to him, and his honest account of how he provoked the second. Boswell was not impressive to look at. Even when he pulled himself together in order to give a portrait painter every encouragement to portray a feudal landlord, he could not banish an expression of uneasiness, such as a feudal landlord accustomed to being pelted with dead cats by his tenantry might wear. Being partially aware of his unimpressiveness, he was afraid that if he allowed his introduction to Johnson to pass without any diversion, Johnson would forget that he was there, and all hope of a closer acquaintance would be gone. This at any rate seems the most reasonable inference from his account of how, as Davies was introducing him, he recollected Johnson's prejudice against the Scots, and exclaimed in agitation, "Don't tell him where I come from." If he had been anxious to conceal his nationality, he would have kept quiet. Davies obliged with "From Scotland," and Boswell added, "Mr. Johnson, I do indeed come from Scotland, but I cannot help it." This speech, he says, was somewhat unlucky, for Johnson, interpreting it not as a statement that Boswell was born in Scotland, but that he had left Scotland to better his fortunes, retorted, "That, Sir, I find, is what a very great number of your countrymen cannot help."

Boswell says that he was a good deal stunned by this stroke; and one may believe him, for Johnson's retort was final, whereas Boswell had expected some pleasantry which would offer him a chance for an engaging rejoinder.

Turning to Davies, Johnson told him that Garrick had refused a free place to Miss Williams, because he knew the house would be full, and a free place would cost him three shillings. Boswell now thrust forward again, but on this occasion he makes no pretence that he interrupted for any reason except to attract Johnson's attention. "Oh, Sir," he cried, "I cannot think Mr. Garrick would grudge such a trifle to you." A second and far heavier blow put Boswell out of action for some time, and when he returned to life he sat quiet, listening to Johnson. Later in the evening Davies left Boswell alone with Johnson, and he ventured an occasional remark, which was civilly received. Davies returned, Boswell outstayed Johnson, and on complaining to Davies of the blows he had received, was comforted with—"Don't be uneasy. I can see he likes you very well."

A week later, encouraged by Davies, Boswell called on Johnson and was disconcerted at the uncouthness of his appearance, his rusty brown suit, his too-small unpowdered wig, his open shirt-neck, his breeches unfastened at the knees, his black-worsted stockings in wrinkles, and his unbuckled shoes. But all these slovenly particularities, he says, were forgotten the moment Johnson began to talk. Although he was friendly and told Boswell that he was obliged to any man who visited him, Boswell called on him only twice between this date, May 24, and the beginning of July. During this period, he tells us, he was occupied by the dissipations of London, which he enjoyed in the company of Wilkes and the satirist Churchill. Casanova had just arrived in London, attracted by the hope of sharing in the good fortune of his old mistress, Thérèse Imer, who, under the name of Madame Cornelis, had established herself as the night-club queen of the age. Wilkes and Casanova met, probably at the entertainments given by Madame Cornelis, and Boswell no doubt accompanied Wilkes, and may have noticed the growing gloom of Casanova, who was finding it impossible to persuade Madame Cornelis that it would be to her advantage to let him share in the profits of her enterprise. Boswell may have also brushed against Casanova in more auspicious surroundings, for Casanova was much pleased with the style in which the better-class London brothels were conducted. A rich man, he says, may sup, bathe, and sleep with a fashionable courtesan for no more than six guineas. A magnificent debauch he calls it, adding that the expense could be reduced to one hundred francs, but economy in pleasure was not to his taste.

The second of Boswell's two meetings with Johnson during these weeks was accidental. He was lunching in an eating-house when Johnson came in, and as he was affable Boswell ventured to ask him to supper that evening at the Mitre. "We had a good supper," Boswell writes, "and port wine, of which he then sometimes drank a bottle. The orthodox High-Church sound of the MITRE—the figure and manner of the celebrated SAMUEL JOHNSON—the extraordinary power and precision of his conversation, and the pride arising from finding myself admitted as his companion, produced a variety of sensations, and a pleasing elevation of mind beyond what I had ever before experienced."

In the course of the meal, Boswell gave Johnson a little sketch of his life, and owned that, in spite of a very strict education in the principles of religion, he had for a time been misled into a certain degree of infidelity, but was now come to a better way of thinking, and was fully satisfied of the truth of the Christian revelation. "Give me your hand!" cried Johnson, "I have taken a liking to you." From religion Boswell passed to his position as the eldest son of a landed proprietor. The advantages of good birth and the necessity of maintaining social distinctions formed a theme which Bos-

well never wearied of introducing in the presence of Johnson. Boswell had a good deal of malice, the revenge of his
mortified vanity. The blows, which from the first moment of
their acquaintance Johnson dealt out to him, necessitated
some kind of reprisal; and even when Johnson was amiable
his massive self-confidence was somewhat galling to Boswell,
who relieved his perhaps hardly conscious annoyance by
pricking Johnson where he expected him to be tender. He
was often successful, and a roar from Johnson rewarded his
dexterity. But although in his youth Johnson had felt his
social inferiority keenly, it is clear that he did not trouble
much about it after he had become famous from Boswell's
repeated failures to provoke him to an explosion against his
social superiors. Whenever Boswell gave voice to his enthusiasm for birth, Johnson took up the theme and complacently
developed it. Once, in the first weeks of their acquaintance,
Boswell said that he considered distinction of rank of such
importance that if he were asked on the same day to dine
with the first Duke in England, and with the first man in
Britain for genius, he would hesitate which to prefer. "If you
were to dine only once," Johnson replied, "and it were never
to be known where you dined, you would choose rather to
dine with the first man for genius; but to gain most respect,
you should dine with the first Duke in England. For nine
people in ten that you meet with would have a higher
opinion of you for having dined with a Duke; and the great
genius himself would receive you better, because you had
been with the great Duke."

On the following day, the subject being introduced again,
Johnson summarized his belief in the necessity of social distinctions in a sentence which shows that his conservatism did

not derive from a belief in the intrinsic merits of an aristocracy, but was based on moral considerations. "There would," he said, "be a perpetual struggle for precedence, were there no fixed invariable rules for the distinction of rank, which creates no jealousy, as it is allowed to be accidental." Only on one occasion did Johnson allow himself even the mildest expression of restiveness under the goadings of his companion. "I have great merit," he once said when Boswell was present, "in being zealous for subordination and the honours of birth; for I can hardly tell who was my grandfather."

Their first supper at the Mitre was followed a few days later by another, at which Goldsmith was present. Johnson had first met Goldsmith two years earlier, and had recently negotiated the sale of *The Vicar of Wakefield* to a bookseller who did not publish it till 1766, by which date, owing to the success of *The Traveller,* Goldsmith was at last well-known to the public. Boswell, who knew Goldsmith slightly, listened deferentially to Johnson's praise of him. "Dr. Goldsmith," said Johnson, "is one of the first men we now have as an author, and he is a very worthy man too. He has been loose in his principles, but he is coming right." Boswell's hostility to Goldsmith has been much exaggerated; and the sketch of Goldsmith which he gives after quoting Johnson's praise shows that he disliked Goldsmith only insofar as Goldsmith reminded him of Boswell. His person, Boswell says, was short, his countenance coarse and vulgar. His mind resembled a fertile but thin soil. There was a quick but not a strong vegetation, of whatever chanced to be thrown upon it. He had, Boswell fears, no settled system of any sort, and his conduct must not therefore be too strictly scrutinized. His affections were social and generous.

During the next few weeks Boswell frequently called on Johnson, and at last received the final proof of Johnson's friendship in an invitation to tea with Miss Williams. "There are few people to whom I take so much as to you," Johnson said to him. Boswell's love of life and inexhaustible interest in everything delighted Johnson. He said they must go together to the Hebrides, and when Boswell described the romantic seat of his ancestors, Johnson exclaimed, "I must be there, Sir, and we will live in the old castle; and if there is not room in it remaining, we will build one."

Boswell was about to set out for Utrecht to study law, having in deference to his father's wishes abandoned his military ambitions. He begged Johnson to advise him about a method of study, and Johnson proposed that they should go to Greenwich for the day, and talk it over. They were having supper together, and afterwards walked down the Strand arm in arm. A prostitute accosted them. "No, no, my girl," said Johnson, "it won't do"; and as he and Boswell walked on, they talked of the wretched life of such women, and agreed that much more misery than happiness is produced by illicit commerce between the sexes.

Two days later they were rowed down to Greenwich, and on arriving Boswell took Johnson's *London* from his pocket, and in a fervent tone recited:

> "On Thames's banks in silent thought we stood:
> Where Greenwich smiles upon the silver flood:
> Pleas'd with the seat which gave Eliza birth,
> We kneel and kiss the consecrated earth."

The business of the day was now entered upon, and Johnson began to outline the methods of study which Boswell was to adopt. Of this discourse Boswell, who had a perfect memory for what interested him, could hardly recall a word. "I recollect with admiration," he says, "an animating blaze of eloquence, which roused every intellectual power in me to the highest pitch, but must have dazzled me so much, that my memory could not preserve the substance of his discourse; for the note which I find of it is no more than this: 'He ran over the grand scale of human knowledge; advised me to select some particular branch to excel in, but to acquire a little of every kind.' "

The day finished with supper at the Turk's Head, during which Boswell surveyed in great detail the history of his family and the extent and population of the family estate. Before they parted, Johnson said he must see Boswell out of England, and a few days later they set out for Harwich in the stage coach. With a journey and congenial society before him, Johnson's high spirits used always to break out. One of their fellow-passengers, a fat elderly gentlewoman, told them that she had done her best to educate her children and had never suffered them to be idle for a moment. "I wish, Madam, you would educate me too," said Johnson; "for I have been an idle fellow all my life . . . and that gentleman there" (pointing at Boswell) "has been idle. He was idle at Edinburgh, his father sent him to Glasgow where he continued to be idle. He then came to London where he has been very idle; and now he is going to Utrecht, where he will be as idle as ever." Boswell, who was seeing himself as an earnest student under the special protection of the great moralist of the age, remonstrated with Johnson as soon as they were alone. "How could you expose me so?" he complained. "Poh, poh! They know nothing about you, and will think of it no more."

The next day they arrived at Harwich, and after a meal at the inn visited a church, where Johnson made Boswell kneel and recommend himself to the protection of his Creator and Redeemer. His high spirits were gone. The prospect of the solitary journey back to London depressed him. "My revered friend," Boswell writes, "walked down with me to the beach, where we embraced and parted with tenderness, and engaged to correspond by letters. I said, 'I hope, Sir, you will not forget me in my absence.' Johnson: 'Nay, Sir, it is more likely you should forget me, than that I should forget you.' As the vessel put out to sea, I kept my eyes upon him for a considerable time, while he remained rolling his majestick frame in his usual manner; and at last I perceived him walk back into the town, and he disappeared."

CHAPTER FIVE

Eccentricities—*Shakespeare*—Mr. and Mrs. Thrale—
Dr. Taylor

(1)

IN spite of the diversion of travel, Johnson was not happy in the first years after his pension. Being released from the necessity to earn a living, he found it harder than ever to keep to a regular programme. His edition of Shakespeare was long overdue, and as he had taken subscriptions for it, his procrastination must have been a permanent source of uneasiness. Apart from his evasion of this duty, he suffered from a general sense of neglecting to make a proper use of his gifts. In talk his combativeness forced him to defend his idleness. When Goldsmith reproached him for not writing, he retorted that he was not obliged to do any more, that no man was obliged to do as much as he could; and he compared himself to a physician who leaves a large London practice for a small practice in the provinces. The good he could do by his conversation, he said, bore the same proportion to the good he could do by his writings as the practice of a physician retired to a small town bore to his practice in a great city. "I wonder, Sir," interjected Boswell, "you have not more pleasure in writing than in not writing." "Sir, you *may* wonder."

In his Journal we learn what he felt when he was alone. "My indolence," he wrote on Easter Day, 1764, "has sunk into grosser sluggishness, and my dissipation spread into wilder negligence. My thoughts have been clouded with sensuality, and, except that from the beginning of this year I have in some measure forborne excess of Strong Drink, my appetites have predominated over my reason. A kind of strange oblivion has overspread me, so that I know not what has become of the last year." A year later he wrote that he had reformed no evil habits since the preceding Easter, that his time had been unprofitably spent, and seemed as a dream that had left nothing behind. His melancholia was intensified by his remorse and became for a short time so acute that his usual anxiety for company left him, and he would not see anyone except his old friend Dr. Adams, who found him sighing, groaning, talking to himself, and restlessly walking from room to room. "I would consent to have a limb amputated," he exclaimed, "to recover my spirits."

Even when he was not suffering from a crisis of this kind, his health, it must be remembered, was always bad. He could seldom get off to sleep before three or four in the morning, and therefore found it very difficult to rise before noon or even later. "I do not remember," he once said, "that since I left Oxford I ever rose early by mere choice, but once or twice at Edial, and two or three times for *The Rambler.*" From this late rising, with its various consequences, sprung much of his remorse. During the week it prevented him from working, and on Sundays it interfered with his attendance at divine service. His remissness in churchgoing, which troubled him perpetually, was also due to his dislike of sermons. It is clear from several passages in his Journal that not even his religion could reconcile him to the necessity of remaining silent while a fellow-creature talked for half or three-quarters of an hour; and he was further exasperated by his deafness. Not only had he to keep quiet, he had to strain his attention to catch what the preacher was saying. He notes brusquely as one of his resolutions to attend the sermon, if he can hear it, unless attention be more troublesome than useful.

This intrusion of his human side upon his religious is also illustrated in an incident which he records at some length in his Journal. Each Easter for several years he had observed a poor man at the Sacrament, and at last he asked the man to come home with him. The man turned out to be a Methodist, full of texts and lacking in intelligence. Johnson began to feel irritable, and his irritation was so much increased by the man twice refusing, doubtless with a pained air, to take wine that he ejected him ("suffered him to go") without the dinner which had been prepared for him. "I am sorry to have been so much disappointed," he notes, and resolves in future to be more tolerant of mean persons who, in spite of indeterminate notions, and perverse or inelegant conversation, may perhaps be doing all they can.

Johnson's eccentricity in the company of others often sprung from a sudden impulse to throw off the oppression which weighed on him in solitude. In 1764, during this period of unusual gloom, he visited his friend Bennet Langton in Lincolnshire, and one day they walked up a very steep hill. On reaching the summit Johnson said that he was going to take a roll down. Langton tried to dissuade him, but he insisted that he had not had a roll for a long time, and meant to have one now. Emptying his pockets of their contents, he laid himself parallel with the edge of the hill, pushed off, and turned over with increasing velocity until he reached the bottom.

Once, in his late fifties, as he was walking with some friends in Gunisbury Park, one of the party pointed to a group of lofty trees and said that when he was a boy he made nothing of climbing the largest of them. "I can swarm it now," exclaimed Johnson, and climbed half-way up before the protests of the others could persuade him to desist. Even more remarkable was the race he ran with a girl during his visit to Devonshire. There was a large lawn outside a room in which he was sitting. Someone observed that it would be very suitable to run a race on, a girl who was present said she could outrun any of the company, and Johnson rose at once and challenged her. "The lady at first had the advantage," Miss Reynolds narrates, "but Dr. Johnson happening to have slippers on much too small for his feet, kick'd them off up into the air, and ran a great length without them, leaving the lady far behind him, and having won the victory he returned, leading her by the hand, with looks of high exultation and delight."

Miss Reynolds, who is our authority for both these stories, was a great friend of Johnson. It was to her that he made one of his wisest observations: Women, he said, were timorous, but were not cautious. Miss Reynolds gives many instances of his peculiarities of manner, which can be accepted as free from exaggeration, for she loved Johnson, and in her quaintly spelt reminiscences of him, tells how when a lady (probably herself) was relating to Johnson that she had seen in a churchyard "a very stricking object of maternal affection, a little verdent flowery monument, raised by the Widow'd Mother over the grave of her only child, she heard him make heavy sighs, indeed sobs, and turning round she saw his Dear Face bathed in tears."

The strange positions in which he would place his feet, she records, were scarcely credible. Sometimes he would make the back part of his heels touch, sometimes his toes, as if endeavouring to form a triangle; and his gestures with his hands were equally strange. He would hold them up with some of his fingers bent, as if he had been seized with the cramp; or he would lift them breast high and revolve them like a jockey urging on his horse. "One Sunday morning," she writes, "as I was walking with him in Twickenham Meadows, he began his antics both with his feet and his hands. . . . I well remember that they were so extraordinary that men, women, and children gathered round him, laughing."

These and other strangenesses in Johnson's behaviour are more clearly understood when placed against the background of his lifelong struggle to preserve his mental balance. Dr. Birkbeck Hill criticizes Boswell for saying that Johnson's merriment was sometimes out of all proportion to its cause; and Max Beerbohm, in his essay on "Laughter," suggests that though Boswell had an exquisitely keen sense of comedy, he could not appreciate imaginative burlesque and anything bordering on nonsense. Whatever may be thought of this judgment on a man capable of asking Johnson what he would do if he were shut up in a castle with a newborn child, it is clear in the two examples of Johnson's disproportionate merriment given by Boswell that Johnson's laughter passed far beyond its occasion even in the first example, rich though it is in humour, and in the second example was a vent for emotions hardly connected with their ostensible cause.

In the first story, Boswell tells how when he and Johnson

were in the Hebrides one of their hosts offered Johnson an island, on condition that he should reside there for three months in each year. Johnson took up the idea, said he would build a house on the island, would fortify it, and have cannon, would plant and would sally out and take the neighbouring isle of Muck. As these fancies crowded upon him, he burst into a fit of laughter, which became wilder and wilder, and from which he could not for some time force himself to desist.

In the second story Boswell narrates that Johnson dined with General Paoli one day, but was so ill that he had to leave. In the evening, though he was still very ill, he visited Mr. Chambers in the Temple. Chambers, to Johnson's growing annoyance, proposed a number of remedies for his indisposition. "Stay till I am well," he at last exclaimed, "and then you shall tell me how to cure myself." The talk (Boswell was present) arrived at the advantages of high birth, and it was on this occasion that Johnson for the first and last time betrayed a slight impatience with this topic. But he recovered himself and began to hold forth on the dignity and propriety of male succession. It happened that Bennet Langton had asked Chambers earlier in the day to draw up his will, in which he left his estate to his three sisters, in preference to a remote male heir. Chambers mentioned this, and Johnson began to laugh. "I dare say he thinks he has done a mighty thing," he exclaimed. "He won't stay till he gets home to his seat in the country to produce this wonderful deed: he'll call up the landlord of the first inn on the road; and after a suitable preface upon mortality and the uncertainty of life, will tell him that he should not delay in making his will . . ." And so, while the company smiled awkwardly, he ran on, rounding off with: "I hope you have had more conscience than to make him say, 'being of sound understanding'! Ha, ha, ha! I hope he has left me a legacy. I'd have his will turned into verse, like a ballad."

Mr. Chambers showed a growing impatience to get rid of Johnson, who left the house still laughing, Boswell with him. Outside the Temple Gate, Boswell narrates, he burst into such a fit of laughter that he appeared to be almost in a convulsion. "In order to support himself, he laid hold of one of the posts at the side of the foot pavement, and sent forth peals so loud, that in the silence of the night his voice seemed to resound from Temple Bar to Fleet ditch."

(2)

For a few months from the beginning of 1766 Johnson for the first and last time managed to rise early. In March he wrote to Bennet Langton that since the New Year he had risen every morning at about eight. "When I was up," he added, "I have done but little; yet it is no slight advancement to obtain for so many hours more, the consciousness of being."

The reason for this burst of energy is unknown, but it is reasonable to suppose that it was largely due to his relief at having at last finished his edition of Shakespeare. Of the pleasure he felt on completing a task which had been on his hands for nine years there is no record either in his private writings or in his talk. When he was alone he was too humble to express delight at anything he had done, and when he was with others he was too arrogant.

How long he took over his *Shakespeare,* whether he

worked at it every now and then during the nine years, or dispatched it in a few months, is not known; nor do we know if there was any special incentive which forced him to complete it. To outside criticism of his dilatoriness he opposed a stubborn front. There is no evidence to show that he was affected even by Churchill's savage attack:

> "He for subscribers baits his hook,
> And takes their cash; but where's the book?
> No matter where; wise fear, we know,
> Forbids the robbing of a foe;
> But what, to serve our private ends,
> Forbids the cheating of our friends?"

Nor did he betray any of the uneasiness he must have felt at neglecting to produce work for which he had been paid in advance. On one occasion a young bookseller who had handed him a subscription asked timidly if he would take the subscriber's address, to insert in the printed list. "I shall print no list of subscribers," Johnson said abruptly, adding blandly after a moment's pause, "Sir, I have two very cogent reasons for not printing any list of subscribers;—one that I have lost all the names, the other, that I have spent all the money."

It was, according to Hawkins, the concern of his intimates for his reputation which finally led to the completion of the work. Reynolds and some of his other friends, Hawkins says vaguely, contrived to entangle him by a wager, or some other pecuniary engagement, to perform his task by a certain time. Johnson's insensitiveness to the opinion of others was largely assumed, and it is more likely that he was stimulated by Churchill than that he allowed himself to be bribed by his friends to do his duty, but probably his chief incentive was the remorse over his indolence revealed in his Journal. The edition when it at last appeared illustrated the full extent of his critical powers. It was not, judged by modern standards, a work of scholarship. Johnson knew little of Shakespeare's fellow-dramatists, and less of the social life of the Elizabethans, and the Elizabethan stage. But he had studied the text of Shakespeare with the energy he always brought to bear when he shook off his inertia. "Not a single passage in the whole work," he wrote, "has appeared to me corrupt, which I have not endeavoured to restore; or obscure, which I have not endeavoured to illustrate."

Yet to labours of this kind he attached little importance in comparison with the delight to be found even in a corrupt and unannotated text of Shakespeare. "Let him that is yet unacquainted with Shakespeare," he says, ". . . read every play from the first scene to the last, with utter negligence of all his commentators. When his fancy is once on the wing, let it not stoop at correction or explanation."

Johnson's love of Shakespeare began in childhood. When he was nine he was reading *Hamlet* in the kitchen, but the Ghost's entrance frightened him, and he ran upstairs and opened the front door to see the people in the street. He that peruses Shakespeare, he wrote of *Macbeth* in later years, looks round alarmed, and starts to find himself alone. *King Lear* affected him even more strongly. "I was many years ago," he says in the preface to his *Shakespeare,* "so shocked by Cordelia's death, that I know not whether I ever endured to read again the last scenes of the play till I undertook to revise them as an editor."

These quotations show how strongly Shakespeare appealed to the imaginative and passionate elements in Johnson's na-

ture. But as these were the elements which he was always trying to suppress, he concentrated both in his talk and in his
writings on the less disturbing side of Shakespeare's genius.
It was doubtful, he once wrote, whether all Shakespeare's
successors had contributed to their country's literature more
maxims of theoretical knowledge, or more rules of practical
prudence. Yet Shakespeare was not sufficiently didactic for
him, and he regretted that his plays were not tracts. From
Shakespeare's writings, he said, a system of social duty may
be selected, for he that thinks reasonably must think morally;
but his precepts and axioms drop casually from him; he
makes no just distribution of good or evil, nor is always careful to show in the virtuous disapprobation of the wicked; he
carries his persons indifferently through right and wrong,
and at the close dismisses them without further care, and
leaves their examples to operate by chance.

Passages like these have obscured Johnson's profound love
of Shakespeare. When he allowed his feelings natural play, he
was carried out of himself alike by Shakespeare's humour and
by his poetry. "But Falstaff, unimitated, inimitable Falstaff,
how shall I describe thee?" he suddenly bursts forth in his
sober comments on *Henry IV;* during his later years, when
he was not disposed to talk, he was often heard to murmur
Claudio's, "Ay, but to die and go we know not where"; and
a few days before his death, when his doctor visited him after
a restless night, he broke out in Macbeth's cry:

> "Can'st thou not minister to a mind diseased;
> Pluck from the memory a rooted sorrow;
> Raze out the written troubles of the brain;
> And, with some sweet oblivious antidote,
> Cleanse the stuff'd bosom of that perilous stuff,
> Which weighs upon the heart?"

Beneath the asperities thrown off in his didactic moments his sense of Shakespeare's greatness was deep and lasting. Once when Mrs. Thrale had taken advantage of his spirit of contradiction to involve him in the assertion that Young had described night more poetically than Shakespeare, he recovered himself and expressed, at Young's expense, his true opinion of Shakespeare: "Young froths, and foams, and bubbles sometimes very vigorously; but we must not compare the noise made by your tea-kettle here with the roaring of the ocean."

The bout of early rising which Johnson reported to Bennet Langton in March 1766, was dwindling by the beginning of May, and he was attacked by another crisis of his melancholia. One day during this attack the Thrales, whom he had known for nearly eighteen months, called on him, and found him on his knees with a clergyman, beseeching God in distracted tones to preserve his reason. When the clergyman had gone Johnson burst into self-condemnation so violent that Thrale involuntarily put his hand to Johnson's mouth to silence him. Thrale left his wife to soothe Johnson, but before going told her to persuade him to join them at Streatham for a long holiday.

(3)

The Thrales had been married nearly three years at this time: Thrale was thirty-eight, his wife twenty-five. The son of a self-made man, who had bought and greatly enlarged a brewery at Southwark, Henry Thrale was educated at Eton and Oxford, and enjoyed a large allowance before he suc-

ceeded to the brewery on his father's death. His character, as
there was nothing original in it, was almost entirely shaped
by his origin and his upbringing. His origin made him attach
the highest importance to rank and fashion, and his upper-
class education and generous allowance enabled him to imitate the models he admired. In his youth he went the grand
tour with the future Lord Westcote, and on his return to
London he was conscientiously high-spirited, cultivating actresses, and indulging in crude practical jokes. On succeed-
ing to his father's business at the age of thirty, he sobered
down, was elected Member of Parliament for the Borough
of Southwark a few years later, and represented the Borough
continuously till a year before his death.

The social obsession of a self-made aristocrat is so intense
that it is difficult to trace the original disposition beneath the
engrafted character. One would expect Thrale, as one of
Johnson's chief friends, to have had many intellectual interests. "It is a great mistake," Johnson said of the Thrales,
"to suppose that she is above him in literary attainments.
She is more flippant; but he has ten times her learning: he is
a regular scholar; but her learning is that of a schoolboy in
one of the lower forms." Of Thrale's culture there is no evidence except this tribute. We know that Thrale listened attentively to Johnson's talk, but, as in the parallel instances of
Levett and Psalmanazar, we have no record of any contribution by Thrale to any of the topics on which Johnson enlarged at his table. Johnson himself realized this, and said
that if Thrale would talk more, his manner would be completely that of a fine gentleman.

Even Thrale's marriage does not allow us any glimpse of
his natural as distinguished from his acquired tastes. The

attraction of Hester Salusbury, his future wife, seems to have consisted chiefly in her ancient lineage. She was the daughter of John Salusbury of Bachygraig, a descendant in the direct line from Thomas Salusbury, a member of an old Welsh family, who was knighted by Henry VII after the battle of Blackheath. John Salusbury, when Thrale appeared as a suitor for Hester, said that he would not have her exchanged for a barrel of porter. He died shortly after foiling Thrale's first attempt, and a year later Thrale and Hester Salusbury were married.

Mrs. Thrale, as her portrait shows, was not beautiful, but she was lively, intelligent, and good-humoured. These qualities were in some degree warped by her loveless marriage, during which she bore twelve children, eight of whom died in childhood. In her middle years she was scatter-brained and exaggerated, characteristics which are present in her account of Johnson; but her long and happy marriage with Piozzi restored to her much of her original charm. In the journal of her tour in Wales, with her husband and Johnson, there is a passage which reveals a nature unusually open to happiness in favouring circumstances, as her second marriage proved. She is describing the drive from St. Albans to Dunstable, through country where she had passed several of her early years, and writes of "emotions perpetually changing, and perpetually strong, every sign, every bush, every stone almost, reminding me of times long passed but not forgotten; of incidents not pleasing in themselves perhaps, but delightful from their connection with youthful gaiety and the remembrance of people now dead, to some of whom I was far more dear than to any now living. Here I hunted with my Uncle, here I fished or walked with my Father, here my

Grandmother reproved my Mother for her too great indulgence of me, here poor dear Lady Salusbury fainted in the coach and charged me not to tell Sir Thomas of the accident lest it should affect him, here we were overturned, and on this place I wrote foolish verses which were praised by my foolisher Friends."

Thrale made no pretence even during his courtship of being in love with her. In her diary she records that he was never alone with her for more than five minutes at any time before the close of their wedding-day. After their marriage, she says, he was not unkind to her; indeed, he was kinder than she had counted on "to a *plain girl,* who had not one attraction in his eyes." It is clear that he valued her as a wife, not as a woman. Little tender of her person, she says, he was very partial to her understanding. The two things he expected from her were to entertain brilliantly and to give him a male heir. The first expectation was fully satisfied, but of the two sons she bore him, the younger died in infancy, and the elder a year later, a blow from which Thrale never recovered.

The first meeting between Johnson and the Thrales, which apparently took place early in 1765, was arranged by Arthur Murphy, who had also been responsible for breaking the offer of the pension to Johnson. Murphy was an old acquaintance of Thrale, so the capture of Johnson was probably planned by Thrale, not by his wife. It was a little over a year since their marriage, and the salon over which Mrs. Thrale was to preside still lacked its celebrities. The other guest of honour at Johnson's first visit to Streatham was James Woodhouse, who by virtue of being a shoemaker was enjoying a fashionable triumph as a poet. Mrs. Montague, the reigning literary hostess of the day, had attached him to her salon as one of her leading lions, but Murphy lured him away for the evening. He did not, however, roar to much effect in the presence of Johnson. "We liked each other so well," Mrs. Thrale writes of Johnson, "that the next Thursday was appointed for the same company to meet, exclusive of the shoemaker, and since then Johnson has remained till this day our constant acquaintance, visitor, companion, and friend."

It was towards the end of June 1766 that Mrs. Thrale, at her husband's suggestion, persuaded Johnson to leave town for a visit to Streatham. This stay, his first long one, lasted till the end of September.

Of Thrale's place at Streatham, which was country at that time, Fanny Burney's sister wrote: "It surpassed all my expectations. The avenue to the house, plantations, etc., are beautiful; worthy of the charming inhabitants. It is a little Paradise, I think. Cattle, poultry, dogs, all running freely about, without annoying each other."

In these surroundings, nursed and petted by Mrs. Thrale, and treated with due respect by Mr. Thrale, Johnson recovered from his attack of melancholia. The task of restoring Johnson to health was not an easy one, Mrs. Thrale says, and it was complicated for her by the mutual hostility of Johnson and her mother, Mrs. Salusbury. Foreign politics, of which she knew nothing except what she learnt from the daily papers, were Mrs. Salusbury's chief interest. Johnson soon lost patience with her agitations over Poland, Russia, and Turkey, and to revenge himself, Mrs. Thrale records, wrote in the newspapers about battles and plots which had no existence. Mrs. Salusbury was furious on finding out that she had been hoaxed, and she and Johnson were not reconciled till her severe illness some years later.

That the great moralist of the age should go to considerable trouble to bamboozle an old lady is an incident which might well ruin its narrator's credit as a truthful historian. Yet the incident is recorded independently by Sir Brooke Boothby, an old Lichfield friend, who heard it from Johnson himself. To cure a lady of his acquaintance of believing everything she read in the papers, Johnson told Boothby, he fabricated a story of a battle between the Russians and Turks; and that it might bear internal evidence of its futility, he laid the scene of the battle at the conflux of the Boristhenes and the Danube, two rivers separated from one another by a hundred leagues. "The lady," Johnson added, "believed the story, and never forgave the deception; the consequence of which was, that I lost an agreeable companion, and she was deprived of an innocent amusement."

This harrying of Mrs. Thrale's mother, as Thrale was unaffected by it, did not prejudice Johnson's position at Streatham, which now became his second home. During the summer months, until Thrale's death sixteen years later, Johnson spent the middle days of each week at Streatham, returning to his household at the week-end to preside at their Sunday dinner. He had his own room at Streatham, and another room at the Thrales' house at Southwark, to which he made frequent visits when they came up to town for the winter.

The later years of his life, he often said, were the happiest. He was famous, he had enough money, and many more friends than in the period of his struggle. But the chief contribution to his happiness was made by the Thrales, and espe-

cially by Mrs. Thrale, although in a letter written to a friend
after his estrangement from her he only names her husband.
"One great abatement of all miseries," he wrote, "was the
attention of Mr. Thrale, which from our first acquaintance
was never intermitted. I passed far the greater part of many
years in his house where I had all the pleasure of riches without the solicitude. He took me into France one year, and into
Wales another, and if he had lived would have shown me
Italy and perhaps many other countries, but he died in the
spring of 'eighty-one, and left me to write his epitaph."

While the Thrales made Johnson happy, he made them
famous. Reynolds, Burke, and Bishop Percy, Goldsmith, Garrick, Dr. Burney, and many others followed Johnson to
Streatham. But where material benefits are regularly conferred, it is impossible for the recipient to preserve his independence completely. The value which Johnson, after his life
of poverty and with his dread of solitude, attached to his
connexion with Streatham was so great that he sacrificed
some of his self-respect to preserve it, and turned a blind eye
on what it was not to his interest to see clearly. In the worst
days of his struggle, with a sick wife to support, Johnson
thrashed the bookseller Tom Osborne for insolence, though
Osborne was giving him work at the time. This ferocity
suited his character better than his playfulness in calling
Thrale "my master" when he wrote to Mrs. Thrale. Although Thrale was nearly twenty years younger than himself, Johnson would allow Thrale to cut him short with:
"There, there, now we have had enough for one lecture, Dr.
Johnson; we will not be upon education any more until after
dinner, if you please." That Johnson suffered this without
protest is in itself sufficient proof of Mrs. Thrale's statement

that his fondness for Thrale had a dash of self-interest.

In one of her marginal notes on Boswell's *Johnson,* Mrs. Thrale comments on a letter from Johnson to Levett during his tour in Wales. "Wales, so far as I have yet seen of it," Johnson wrote, "is a very beautiful and rich country." Mrs. Thrale remarks, "Yet, to please Mr. Thrale, he feigned abhorrence of it." Against this must be set her note on Boswell's suggestion that Johnson's intimacy with the Thrales was not without some degree of restraint. "What restraint can he mean?" Mrs. Thrale exclaims. "Johnson kept everyone else under restraint." But the contradiction is only apparent. Johnson was far too autocratic and too famous to be treated like a dependant. He used the Thrales' house as if it had been his own, and never scrupled to keep Mrs. Thrale up till two or three in the morning to enliven his melancholy and make tea for him. But he realized Thrale's love of authority—"I know no man," he said, "who is more master of his wife and family than Thrale. If he but holds up his finger, he is obeyed"—and he humoured it at Mrs. Thrale's expense, if not much at his own. As it was not to his advantage to recognize her unhappiness with her husband, he ignored it so resolutely that when Thrale died he wrote to her that God had given her happiness in marriage, to a degree of which, without personal knowledge, he would have thought the description fabulous—a remark which can be explained only by the seldom realized truth that those we know longest we often know least, and that a man will frequently understand a casual acquaintance better than the wife or friend whom his affection, vanity, or self-interest show to him not as they are but as he wishes them to be.

The story of Thrale's relations with Sophia Streatfield,

which developed under Johnson's eyes, illustrates both what Mrs. Thrale had to put up with, and what Johnson was able to ignore for the sake of his own peace of mind. After the death of his heir in 1776, Henry Thrale began to break up, and in his last three or four years found his only happiness in over-eating and in an attachment to a pretty widow, Sophia Streatfield, described by Mrs. Thrale as "the ivory-necked Sophia, who could weep at will." The affair was what is called innocent, and caused the maximum of discomfort to everyone concerned, except Sophia, who treated flirtation with married men as an art, and numbered bishops and East India Company directors among her victims. Thrale, whose artificial reserve was disintegrating under the strain of advancing years and grief for his son's death, was overpowered by her charm. "She is very pretty," Mrs. Thrale wrote, "very gentle, soft, and insinuating; hangs about him, dances round him, cries when she parts from him, squeezes his hand slyly, and with her sweet eyes full of tears looks so fondly in his face—and all for love of me as she pretends. . . . A man must not be a *man*, but an *it*, to resist such artillery."

That no scandal should attach to his adoration of Sophia, Thrale used to leave his carriage at his sister's door in Hanover Square, when he called on Sophia near by; and he required Mrs. Thrale to safeguard Sophia's reputation still further by having her constantly in their house, and accepting her as the godmother to one of the children. Mrs. Thrale bore this patiently on the whole, but on one occasion she lost her temper. Thrale was giving a large dinner-party at Streatham. Sophia was present, and Johnson and Burke sat on either side of Mrs. Thrale. The attention which Thrale paid to Sophia, to the neglect of everyone else, began to get on the nerves of his wife, who was near a confinement, and in unusually low spirits; and when Thrale brusquely requested her to change places with Sophia, who was exposed to a draught and felt a sore throat coming on, Mrs. Thrale burst into tears, exclaimed that perhaps ere long the lady might be at the head of Mrs. Thrale's table without displacing the mistress of the house, and ran out of the room.

After dinner Johnson and Burke went to the drawing-room, where they found Mrs. Thrale. On seeing them, she says, she resolved to give them both a "jobation," but addressed herself to Johnson alone. Had he noticed what had passed, she asked, and did he think, allowing for the state of her nerves, that she was much to blame? "Why, possibly not," Johnson replied. "Your feelings were outraged." "Yes, they were," Mrs. Thrale retorted; "and I cannot help remarking with what blandness and composure you *witnessed* the outrage. Had this transaction been told of others, your anger would have known no bounds; but, towards a man who gives good dinners, etc., you were meekness itself!"

The great Christian sage, and the future champion of the oppressed millions of India, looked foolish and said nothing.

After Thrale's death, Johnson wrote of him to a friend as "a man whose eye for fifteen years had scarcely been turned upon me but with respect or tenderness." The "scarcely" implies an unconscious doubt about the quality of Thrale's respect and tenderness. The scene which has just been narrated does not suggest much respect, and the fact that Thrale left Johnson only two hundred pounds, instead of the substantial annuity which everyone had anticipated, does not suggest much tenderness.

(4)

The chief happiness of Johnson's later years, and therefore of his whole life, came from his friendship with Mrs.
Thrale. Miss Reynolds tells a story which illustrates both
Mrs. Thrale's good-humoured forbearance with him and his
roughness towards her concealing deep affection. One day at
her own table, Miss Reynolds records, he spoke to Mrs.
Thrale with such rudeness that everyone was surprised she
should bear it so placidly. One of the guests, probably Miss
Reynolds herself, expressed her astonishment to Mrs. Thrale
later, but Mrs. Thrale only said, "Oh! Dear good man!"
Touched by Mrs. Thrale's generosity, the lady reported to
Johnson both her own criticism of him and Mrs. Thrale's
reply. "He seem'd much delighted with this intelligence,"
Miss Reynolds says, "and sometime after, as he was lying back
in his chair, seeming to be half-asleep, but more evidently
musing on this pleasing incident, he repeated in a loud whisper, 'Oh! Dear good man!' "

Mrs. Thrale, easy-going, vivacious, and physically slight
and quick, attracted Johnson as his opposite in every respect.
Once when he was ill, and more than usually obsessed with
his horror of death, she appeared before him in a dark gown,
which his bad sight mistook for grey. "Why do you delight,"
he growled, "thus to thicken the gloom of misery that sur-
rounds me? Is not here sufficient accumulation of horror
without anticipated mourning?" Mrs. Thrale, drawing back
the curtain to let the light fall on her dress, showed him that
it was purple mixed with green. His voice changed, and he
said amiably, "Well, well, you little creatures should never

wear that sort of clothes; they are unsuitable in every way. What! have not all insects gay colours?"

When he was away from Streatham, on holiday at Lichfield, Ashbourne, or Oxford, he wrote to her constantly, and during his tour in the Hebrides his letters to her form a complete journal of his expedition. For what Wordsworth calls "the pleasure which there is in life itself" Johnson had a natural capacity which his melancholia and his circumstances had combined to stifle till he met Mrs. Thrale. In his letters to her it stirs at times, not very buoyantly, yet enough to show how it might have flourished in other conditions. A letter which he wrote to her from Ashbourne, Dr. Taylor's home, in the summer of 1771, illustrates the kind of vivacity she roused in him. "Last Saturday," he writes, "I came to Ashbourne; the dangers or the pleasures of the journey I have at present no disposition to recount; else might I paint the beauties of my native plains; might I tell of 'the smiles of nature, and the charms of art': else might I relate how I crossed the Staffordshire Canal, one of the great efforts of human labour, and human contrivance; which, from the bridge on which I viewed it, passed away on either side, and loses itself in distant regions, uniting waters which nature had divided, and dividing lands which nature had united. I might tell how these reflections fermented in my mind till the chaise stopped at Ashbourne, at Ashbourne in the Peak. Let not the name of the Peak terrify you; I have never wanted strawberries and cream. The great bull has no disease but age. I hope in time to be like the great bull; and hope you will be like him too a hundred years hence."

This great bull, which Mrs. Thrale is to resemble if she lives long enough, and which was for some years the chief pride of the cattle-breeding Taylor, thrusts himself insistently into Johnson's correspondence with Mrs. Thrale. Before he saw it he promised to ascertain its dimensions for her, and after he had seen it he announced that it was very great indeed. In the following year he reported that the great bull and his four sons were all well, and that care was being taken of the breed. Another year passed, and he informed her that the bulls and cows, if there was any change, were growing bigger. A visitor tells Taylor that he has seen a bull superior to the great bull in size, and some months later Johnson writes, "We yet hate the man that had seen a bigger bull." In a letter condoling with Mrs. Thrale on the illness of her mother, he inserts the cheering news that the great bull is well.

It is in the earlier years of their correspondence that Johnson is most vivacious. Here is a little mock-heroic picture of himself and his black equerry: "This night, at nine o'clock, Sam. Johnson and Francis Barber Esquires, set out in the Lichfield stage; Francis is indeed rather upon it. What adventures we may meet with, who can tell?" "This little dog does nothing," he writes of himself in 1768, "but I hope he will mend; he is now reading 'Jack the Giant-Killer' "; and after an illness he says that he is longing to come to Streatham, and bursts out, "And hey, boys, up we go!"

The conflict in his nature between his desire to be sympathized with and his aversion to exposing his troubles may be seen in many of the letters. He cannot refrain from enumerating his ailments. When he has an attack of rheumatism, he must tell her, but he does not dwell on it; and he is understandably concise about his vexatious flatulence. His constant melancholy is only hinted at, in occasional sentences which owe their pathos to their reserve. "Tomorrow and tomorrow —a few designs and a few failures, and the time of designing will be past." From Lichfield he writes, "I took a walk in quest of juvenile images," and tells her on another occasion that everything in Lichfield recalls to his remembrance years in which he proposed what he had not done, and promised himself pleasure which he had not found.

Another reason for his reserve was his fear of wearying her. His overbearing nature was subdued in solitude, and distance made him more understanding and less exacting. He knew that human beings easily tire of one another. "I came away on Wednesday," he wrote to Mrs. Thrale of a visit to Dr. Taylor, "leaving him, I think, in a disposition of mind not very uncommon, at once weary of my stay and grieved at my departure." Partly to combat the fatigue his affection might cause her, and partly from spontaneous sympathy, he interested himself in everything that concerned her. Once when two of her children were ill at Kensington, he went to see them and reported to her that he found them indeed a little spotted with their disorder, but as brisk and gay as health and youth could make them. "I took a paper of sweetmeats, and spread them on the table. They took great delight to show their governess the various animals that were made of sugar; and when they had eaten as much as was fit, the rest were laid up for tomorrow."

His attention to Mrs. Thrale's children was not merely for her sake. Once in conversation he said that he had never wished to have a child of his own, but it was his habit to disclaim desires which he had been forced to repress. He loved children, was always careful not to offend them, and used to try to win their affection with sweets and fairy stories. Boswell tells, but with less than his usual skill, for one would like to know the effect on the child, how Johnson during their Scottish tour talked to a little girl, and, representing himself as a giant, said in a hollow voice that he lived in a cave, and had a bed in the rock, and would take her with him, and she should have a little bed cut opposite to his.

Johnson's letters to Mrs. Thrale's eldest daughter, Hester, whom he called Queeney, have recently been published for the first time. Queeney never wrote to Johnson either as often or at as great length as he desired. When Queeney was small, Mrs. Thrale was partly to blame for this. "Mama knows I would have written sooner," Queeney, aged eight, explains, "but she said you would not be troubled with no more of my stuff." "Mama," Johnson wrote to her on another occasion, "used us both very sorrily when she hindered you from writing to me. She does not know how much I should love to read your letters, if they were a little longer. . . . You said nothing of Lucy, I suppose she is grown a pretty good scholar and a very good playfellow; after dinner we shall have good sport playing all together, and we will none of us cry."

Some years later, when she was fifteen, she wrote to a friend: "Dr. Johnson gives us a Latin lesson every morning. What progress we may make in this most learned scheme I know not, but as I have always told you, I am sure I fag more from fear of disgrace than from hope of profit." To Queeney, Johnson was the old bore who had been about the place ever since she could remember, and all his attempts to amuse and charm her were useless. "It is well for me," he wrote when she was nearly sixteen, "that a Lady so celebrated as Miss Thrale, can find time to write to me. I will recompense your condescension with a maxim. Never treat old friends with neglect however easily you may find new." He continued with a logical demonstration that her affection for him must be proportionate to the length of time she had known him. "You must already have begun to observe that you love a book, or a box, or an instrument that you have had a great part of your life, because it brings a great part of your life back to your view." The argument was wasted on her, and two years later he told her humbly that she was very kind to write to him.

Once the novelty of being on intimate terms with the great man had worn off, the Thrales, parents and children alike, tolerated rather than enjoyed Johnson. As early as 1772, Johnson wrote to Mrs. Thrale from Ashbourne: "So many days and never a letter! . . . And I have been hoping and hoping, but you are so glad to have me out of your mind." After the Welsh tour in 1774, which lasted from the beginning of July to the end of September, the tone of Johnson's letters to Mrs. Thrale is much less lively than in the earlier years of their acquaintance, evidence that he felt, even if he would not acknowledge to himself, a change in the atmosphere of their relations.

Three months cooped up with Thrale and Johnson had worn Mrs. Thrale out, and when she learnt at the end of the tour that she was to return not to Streatham, but to Southwark, she wrote in her journal: "I thought to have lived at Streatham in quiet and comfort, have kissed my children and cuffed them by turns, and had a place always for them to play in, and here I must be shut up in that odious dungeon, where nobody will come near me, the children are to be sick for want of air, and I am never to see a face but Mr. Johnson's. Oh, what a life that is! and how truly I abhor it!"

(5)

After the Thrales, Dr. Taylor of Ashbourne provided the chief alleviation of Johnson's loneliness during his later years. Taylor, a justice of the peace, and a breeder of cattle, was a typical parson-squire, with an income derived from a good property and from several livings. Livings and preferments, Johnson once wrote to Mrs. Thrale, ran in Taylor's head as if he were in want with twenty children. As he had little in common with Johnson, their intimacy puzzled Johnson's friends. Reynolds's explanation was that Johnson understood he was to be Taylor's heir, but such a motive for enduring boredom would have weighed less with Johnson than with Reynolds. Johnson and Taylor had been at Lichfield school together, and Johnson clung to old associations and the friends of his youth. Once when he and Boswell were at Lichfield, he invited an old schoolfellow, Henry Jackson, to dinner. Boswell describes Jackson as a low man, dull and untaught, dressed in a coarse grey coat, black waistcoat, greasy leather breeches, and a yellow uncurled wig, and betraying in his complexion a fondness for drink. The talk entered on a new scheme for dressing leather, by which Jackson hoped to make a little money, and Johnson listened with close attention and offered several suggestions. Jackson died in the following year, and Johnson wrote to Boswell that it was a loss which could not be repaired: "The friends which merit or usefulness can procure us, are not able to supply the place of old acquaintance, with whom the days of youth may be retraced, and those images revived which gave the earliest delight."

Of the sincerity of his attachment to Taylor Johnson gave

a strong proof, with which Taylor could perhaps have dispensed, by getting him out of bed on the night when Mrs. Johnson died. There is no evidence that Johnson ever applied to Taylor for help during the twenty-five years of struggle before his pension, but when he was freed from money troubles he looked forward to a renewal of their old friendship, and in 1765 reproached Taylor for not asking him down to Ashbourne: "I do not know but I may come, invited or uninvited," he wrote, "and pass a few days with you in August or September, unless you send me a prohibition, or let me know that I shall be unsupportably burthensome." He does not, however, seem to have visited Ashbourne before 1769, after which year he went there almost annually till his death. Both heavy and indolent men, he and Taylor endured the boredom of each other's company with a tranquillity which was perhaps never ruffled except when Boswell visited Ashbourne. Taylor was as strongly Whig as Johnson was strongly Tory, and one evening, with what preliminary encouragement from Boswell he does not record, a violent argument sprang up between them about the feeling of the nation towards the House of Stuart. Taylor, says Boswell, was roused to a pitch of bellowing.

In Boswell's absence Taylor was not an exciting companion. "I love him," Johnson said to Boswell during this visit, "but I do not love him more; my regard for him does not increase. As it is said in the Apocrypha, 'His talk is of bullocks'; I do not suppose he is very fond of my company. His habits are by no means sufficiently clerical: this he knows that I see; and no man likes to live under the eye of perpetual disapprobation."

Taylor on his side may have felt that it was unfair to be

blamed for luxurious living by someone who was sharing the luxury he disapproved. Johnson and Boswell were fetched to Ashbourne from Lichfield in a large, roomy post-chaise drawn by four stout, plump horses, and the amenities they found on their arrival were of the most varied order. Everything around Dr. Taylor, Mrs. Thrale records, was both elegant and splendid. He had a magnificent pew in the church; his rooms were hung with fine paintings; he had a glorious harpsichord on which a youth from the village used to perform; there were deer in his paddock, pheasants in his menagerie, and a waterfall at the foot of his garden; he had the best coach horses in the county and the largest horned cattle; his table was liberally spread, and his wines were of many kinds, all excellent.

In 1763 Dr. Taylor had a quarrel with his wife which ended in a permanent separation. During the crisis of the quarrel he wrote to Johnson for advice, and Johnson's replies show, like his views on the relations of parents and children, how mistaken is the popular idea of him, based on an occasional explosion in talk, as a bigoted champion of social conventions and the established order. A profound individualist at heart, he believed that marriage, like the Sabbath, was made for man, not man for marriage; he valued institutions because they were good for human beings, not human beings because they were good for institutions; and where the rights of the individual clashed with the claims of the social system he supported the rights of the individual.

In the pages of Boswell, it is true, he often steps forward as the champion of the conventions; but the hidden hand of Boswell, goading Johnson for his own diversion and at the same time anxious to be strengthened in his uncertain hold on conduct, is perceptible on each occasion. "This is miserable stuff, Sir," Johnson once roared at Boswell. "To the contract of marriage, besides the man and woman, there is a third party —Society; and if it be considered as a vow—God: and, therefore, it cannot be dissolved by their consent alone. Laws are not made for particular cases, but for men in general." This explosion was provoked by Boswell inquiring whether a woman of his acquaintance, whose husband was frequently unfaithful, was justified in considering herself as freed from conjugal obligations. But when Taylor appealed to Johnson for his advice on the breakdown of an unsuitable marriage, Johnson dealt with the question simply as it affected the two persons concerned.

As Dr. Taylor's letters have not been preserved, the story of his quarrel with his wife must be deduced from Johnson's replies. It seems that Mrs. Taylor ran away from Ashbourne in the company of a woman friend, and raised her relations against her husband with the story of her wrongs. These included a charge against Dr. Taylor of misconduct with a certain Hannah, apparently one of the servants at Ashbourne. "The tale of Hannah," Johnson writes, "I suppose to be false, not that if it be true it will justify her violence and precipitation." He advises Taylor not to communicate with his wife's brother. It was for him to write to Taylor, who had been ill-treated by his sister. Taylor, he adds, had been too submissive to his wife's relations in the past, and ought to take this opportunity of asserting himself, though not at the risk of making a reconciliation impossible, since if there were any hope of living happily or decently, cohabitation would be the most reputable for both. To this hope Johnson does not recur after receiving fuller information about the attitude of Mrs. Taylor and her supporters; and he writes a letter for Taylor which he trusts will have the effect of reducing Mrs. Taylor and her friends to moderate and reasonable terms by showing what slight account Taylor makes of their menaces.

After some months an agreement, involving a permanent separation, was arrived at, and Johnson wrote to congratulate Taylor upon this happy end to so vexatious an affair.

The individualism of Puritan morality, in its highest representatives, is forcibly illustrated by the attitude towards marriage of the chief Puritan names in English literature. Milton advocated easier divorce, Bunyan showed Christian leaving his wife and children, and Johnson wrote to Taylor: "Any incident that makes a man the talk and spectacle of the world without any addition to his honour is naturally vexatious, but talks and looks are all the evils which this domestick revolution has brought upon you. I knew that you and your wife lived unquietly together, I find the provocations were greater than I had known, and do not see what you have to regret but that you did not separate in a very short time after you were united."

CHAPTER SIX

Boswell's *Life of Johnson*

(1)

EARLY in 1766, some months before the Thrales took Johnson to Streatham, Boswell returned from the Continent, where he had been for two and a half years.

The three great events of his travels had been his meetings with Rousseau, Voltaire, and Paoli. Rousseau he had tracked to his retreat at Motiers, at the foot of the Jura. "I am an ancient Scots gentleman. You know my rank. I am twenty-four years old. You know my age," he wrote to Rousseau. ". . . I present myself, Sir, as a man of singular merit, a man with a feeling heart, a spirit keen yet melancholy. . . . Open your door then, Sir, to a man who dares to assure you that he is worthy of entering. Have confidence in a singular visitor. You will not repent of it. . . ."

After five visits to Rousseau, who at last, fixed by Boswell's stern eye, confessed that he was proud to be a Christian, Boswell left for Voltaire's château at Ferney, where a stupendous struggle, from which Voltaire tried to escape by feigning a swoon, ended in Voltaire admitting his veneration for the Supreme Being. From Ferney, after dropping a line to Rousseau to inform him that Voltaire was the most brilliant of talkers, Boswell went on to Italy. "I am no libertine, and have a moral certainty of suffering no harm in Italy," he had written to a friend a little earlier. At Turin, Rome, and Naples, he saw a good deal of Wilkes, who had been outlawed from England after his expulsion from the House of Commons. The chastity which Boswell had promised himself in Italy was prejudiced by his association with Wilkes, to whom he wrote after they had parted: "Oh, John Wilkes, thou gay, learned, and ingenious private gentleman, thou thoughtless infidel, good without principle, wicked without malevolence, let Johnson teach thee the road to rational virtue and noble felicity."

Rousseau had given Boswell a letter of introduction to Paoli, the leader of the Corsicans in their struggle for independence against Genoa. To leave Italy for an unexplored island was a bold enterprise, but Boswell undertook it, and found himself at last in the presence of Paoli. "I was of the belief he might be an impostor," Paoli told Fanny Burney many years later. ". . . I supposed he was an espy; for I look away from him, and in a moment I look again, and I behold his tablets. Oh! he was to the work of writing down all I say. Indeed I was angry. But soon I discover he was no impostor and no espy; and I only find I was myself the monster he had come to discern. Oh, Boswell is a very good man; I love him indeed; so cheerful! so gay! so pleasant!"

The weeks Boswell spent with Paoli and his men were perhaps the happiest in his life. In Corsican dress, and armed with two pistols, the gift of Paoli, he lived in "a luxury of noble sentiment," dreaming of an alliance between Corsica and England, a strict union in commerce and in war, to be negotiated by himself.

From Corsica he returned to England through Paris, where he found Thérèse Levasseur, Rousseau's housekeeper and mistress. Rousseau had just left Paris for England with Hume. Thérèse was to join him there, and was glad to accept Boswell's escort. She was forty-one at this date, Boswell was twenty-five, and when in the course of their journey Boswell, nerving himself to the assault with two bottles of wine, overcame such resistance as she offered, he was much chagrined at her verdict that his advantage over Rousseau in age was more than counterbalanced by Rousseau's advantage over him in art.

As soon as he reached London, Boswell called on Johnson, and was struck by the roughness of his manners after the studied, smooth, complying habits to which he had become accustomed on the Continent. That his travels made him feel a certain superiority to the stay-at-home Johnson, and that he kept on insinuating this superiority until Johnson's patience at last gave out, appears between the lines of his narrative. Throughout his relations with Johnson, Johnson's sudden roars, invariably recorded with surprise by Boswell, were usually due to a stealthy application from picador Boswell's lance.

At their first meeting Boswell referred to his talk with Voltaire, and said that he intended to publish an account of his Corsican experiences. Johnson heard the name of Voltaire without impatience, and encouraged the Corsican project. At their next meeting Boswell spoke of his visit to Rousseau in his wild retreat and of the pleasant hours he had passed with Mr. Wilkes in Italy. Johnson began to show restiveness. "You have kept very good company abroad," he growled, "Rousseau and Wilkes!" Boswell expressed wonder at this reflection on Rousseau. Did Johnson really think Rousseau a bad man? Johnson's famous retort has often been quoted as an example of his narrow bigotry: "Rousseau, Sir, is a very bad man. I would sooner sign a sentence for his transportation, than that of any felon who has gone from the Old Bailey these many years. Yes, I should like to have him work in the plantations." But if Boswell had put his mind to it, he could have made Johnson consign St. Francis of Assisi to the plantations, and the Venerable Bede to the gallows. Although connected with his nervous dislike of unorthodox speculation, Johnson's explosion against Rousseau is interesting chiefly as a tribute to Boswell's skill as a picador; and the same interest attaches to his second explosion, when Boswell asked him whether he thought Rousseau as bad as Voltaire: "Sir, it is difficult to settle the proportion of iniquity between them."

Corsica, too, was laboured by Boswell to Johnson's growing impatience. Boswell was overjoyed at finding an object which he imagined would fix his wandering mind, and employ all his faculties. Chatham, a week or two after Boswell reached London, received him as the envoy of Paoli, and for a time Chatham and Paoli overshadowed Johnson. During the next two years he hoped that a liberated Corsica would be his memorial in the history of mankind. "Could your Lordship," he wrote to Chatham, "find time to honour me now and then with a letter? I have been told how favourably your Lordship has spoken of me. To correspond with a Paoli and a Chatham is enough to keep a young man ever ardent in the pursuit of virtuous fame." Nor was his zeal exhausted in words. While he was addressing Chatham in this strain, he was persuading Scotsmen to subscribe to the purchase of artillery for Corsicans, and in the August of 1767 he sent seven hundred pounds' worth of ordnance to Paoli.

"Mind your own affairs, and leave the Corsicans to theirs,"

Johnson wrote to Boswell in August 1766, and nearly two years later he expressed a wish that Boswell would empty his head of Corsica. "My noble-minded friend," Boswell replied, "do you not feel for an oppressed nation struggling to be free? . . . Empty my head of Corsica! Empty it of honour, empty it of humanity, empty it of friendship, empty it of piety! No, while I live, Corsica and the cause of the brave islanders shall ever employ much of my attention, shall ever interest me in the sincerest manner."

What Johnson thought of this exhortation to live up to Boswell is not known. Often one can only guess how Boswell's extravagances struck him, but it is important to realize that Boswell's portrait of Johnson reveals Boswell's effect on Johnson as well as Johnson's effect on Boswell. Though Boswell did not invent Johnson's irritability, he drew it out, and gave it a disproportionate place in the Life. But his goading of Johnson, though partly due to malice, was chiefly due to his desire to see Johnson perform. "Curiosity," Mrs. Thrale said, "carried Boswell further than it ever carried any mortal breathing. He cared not what he provoked so as he saw what such a one would say or do." Yet if Johnson would perform without provocation, Boswell was content to watch without interfering. Frequently, too, his provocations were unintentional, and his pleasure in their results much qualified by the punishment they brought upon his head.

The scenes in Boswell's Life may therefore be grouped in three categories: those which he provoked intentionally, those which he provoked unintentionally, and those which he absorbed as a disinterested spectator. To examine these categories separately is helpful to a clearer understanding both of Johnson and of Boswell.

(2)

Boswell's attempts to provoke Johnson by reminding him of his low birth were, as we have seen, uniformly unsuccessful. But by forcing Johnson to exaggerate his adherence to what Boswell calls the grand scheme of subordination, they have conveyed a distorted idea of Johnson's Toryism as though there were something mystical in his respect for aristocracy. The respect he expressed was in essence a form of moral discipline, designed to mortify his own aggressiveness and desire for worldly distinction. Brains, except as a means to power, have always been of small importance to aristocracies. Johnson realized this, and avoided high society. "Great lords and great ladies," he said, "don't love to have their mouths stopped." There is a note of regret here, as if he would have valued a position in which he could have said his say to the first Duke in England, and to such a position he could have risen, had not his capacity for domination and his practical ability been impeded by his constitutional indolence and neutralized by his higher qualities. His great and rapid success on *The Gentleman's Magazine* and his abrupt renunciation of his success suggest a Cromwell with a conscience instead of a mouth full of texts. He may have felt the affinity, for though he hated Cromwell's politics he was so much interested in him as a man that he thought of writing his life. It would be highly curious, he said, to trace his extraordinary rise to the supreme power from so obscure a beginning.

Johnson's regret for power did not escape Boswell. He had undoubtedly, Boswell says, often speculated on the possibility of his supereminent powers being rewarded in this country by the highest powers of the State. That Johnson did not wish to be reminded of what he had missed was also clear to Boswell, who narrates how, when Sir William Scott remarked that had Johnson become a lawyer he might have been Lord Chancellor of Great Britain, attained to the dignity of the peerage, and revived the extinct title of Lichfield, Johnson exclaimed in an angry tone: "Why will you vex me by suggesting this, when it is too late?"

On two occasions directly, and on one occasion obliquely, Boswell aimed at this sore point, scoring two hits and one miss. The first of his direct aims was adroitly evaded by Johnson. Was he not dissatisfied, Boswell asked him, with having so small a share of wealth, and none of those distinctions in the State which are the objects of ambition? He had only a pension of three hundred a year. Why was he not in such circumstances as to keep a coach? Why had he not some considerable office? "Sir," Johnson replied, "I have never complained of the world; nor do I think that I have reason to complain. It is rather to be wondered at that I have so much. My pension is more out the usual course of things than any instance I have known. . . ."

In the year before Johnson's death, when his health was breaking up, Boswell tried again. He was having tea with Johnson and Mrs. Desmoulins, and "She and I," he narrates, "talked before him on a topic which he had once borne patiently from me when we were by ourselves—his not complaining of the world, because he was not called to some great office, nor had attained to great wealth." Johnson flew into a violent passion, and commanded Boswell and Mrs. Desmoulins to have done. Nobody, he cried, had a right to talk in this manner, to bring before a man his own character and the events of his life. He had never sought the world, and the world was not to seek him. It was rather wonderful, he said, snatching at the consolation he had applied to the wound before, that the world had done so much for him.

Boswell's oblique attack drew Johnson even more successfully. Speaking of Clive, Johnson said that he had acquired his fortune by such crimes that his consciousness of them impelled him to cut his own throat. But, Boswell suggested, may Clive not, as Dr. Robertson held, have cut his throat because he was weary of still life; little things not being sufficient to move his great mind? The implication that everyday existence was interesting enough for Johnson, but not interesting enough for Clive, was not lost on Johnson, who roared: "Nay, Sir, what stuff is this! You had no more this opinion after Robertson said it than before. I know nothing more offensive than repeating what one knows to be foolish things, by way of continuing a dispute, to see what a man will answer,—to make him your butt!" "My dear Sir," protested Boswell, "I had no such intentions as you seem to suggest; I had not indeed. Might not this nobleman have felt everything 'weary, stale, flat, and unprofitable,' as Hamlet says?" To Johnson when roused a Shakespeare was as slight an impediment as a Robertson. "Nay, if you are to bring in gabble, I'll talk no more. I will not, upon my honour."

"My readers," says Boswell, "will decide upon this dispute."

Johnson's horror of death was another temptation which Boswell was unable to resist. Once when he and Johnson were alone, Boswell remarked that Hume (one of Johnson's chief aversions) had told him he was no more uneasy to think he should not be after this life than that he had not been before he began to exist. "Sir, if he really thinks so, his perceptions are disturbed; he is mad: if he does not think so, he lies." But Foote, Boswell urged, had assured him that when he was very ill he was not afraid to die. Foote was a comic actor, yet Johnson remained calm, replying: "It is not true, Sir. Hold a pistol to Foote's breast, or to Hume's breast, and threaten to kill them, and you'll see how they would behave." Boswell tried again. Might one not, he inquired, fortify one's mind for the approach of death? It was wrong of him, he confesses, to bring before Johnson's view what he looked upon with such horror; and he reveals his understanding of Johnson's attitude to death by comparing his mind to a vast amphitheatre, in the centre of which stood his judgment combating, like a gladiator, the apprehension that crowded round him. Yet Johnson still kept his temper. "No, Sir, let it alone," he said. "It matters not how a man dies, but how he lives. The act of dying is not of importance, it lasts so short a time. A man knows it must be so, and submits. It will do him no good to whine." Boswell persisted, with what arguments he does not record, until at last Johnson, who had grown more and more agitated, showed him out of the house, calling after him: "Don't let us meet tomorrow."

Boswell went home exceedingly uneasy, he says, all the harsh observations he had ever heard made upon Johnson's character crowding into his mind.

A few months before Johnson's death, when he was at Oxford with Boswell, Dr. Adams expressed a wish that Johnson would compose some family prayers. This was an innocent enough wish, but there was something in it which touched Johnson's secret terrors and therefore invited a display of

importunity from Boswell. "We all now gathered about him,"
Boswell says, "and two or three of us at a time joined in
pressing him to execute this plan. He seemed to be a little
displeased at our importunity, and in great agitation called
out, 'Do not talk thus of what is so awful. I know not what
time God will allow me in this world. There are many things
which I wish to do.' " Some of the company still persevered.
"Let me alone," Johnson cried, "let me alone; I am overpowered," and, putting his hands before his face, he rested
his head for some time on the table.

Boswell's attempts to draw Johnson on the relations of
the sexes were less successful. In the first weeks of their
acquaintance Johnson and Boswell agreed that much more
misery than happiness is produced by illicit commerce between the sexes. This was Johnson's real view, but when he
knew Boswell better he adopted a more worldly tone, partly
in reaction from his severity in practice, and partly to foil
Boswell's hope of an outburst from the great moralist. Between a man and his wife, a husband's infidelity was nothing,
he once said, in a conversation which Boswell printed and
then expurgated, and which has recently been given in full
in *Life and Letters*. "Wise married women," Johnson continued, "don't trouble themselves about infidelity in their
husbands; they detest a mistress, but don't mind a whore. My
wife told me I might lye with as many women as I pleased,
provided I *loved* her alone." These liberal sentiments surprised Boswell, who began to wonder if he had not overrated
Johnson's virtue. But when he asked Johnson whether a man
might do as he pleased, if his wife refused his embraces,
Johnson replied: "Nay, Sir, this is wild indeed (smiling);

you must consider that fornication is a crime in a single man; and you cannot have more liberty by being married."

It is needless to discuss whether Johnson really believed infidelity in a husband to be consistent with his definition of marriage as the most solemn league of perpetual friendship; and though, when his wife told him he might lie with other women, he may not have realized that she spoke from uneasiness at the difference in age between them, yet it is this uneasiness he tries to allay in his only extant letter to her: "Be assured, my dear Girl, that I have seen nobody in these rambles upon which I have been forced that has not contributed to confirm my esteem and affection for thee."

Johnson as man of the world, instead of moralist, appears again in a discussion between him and Boswell on the reason why young women marry. "You will recollect," Johnson remarks, "my saying to some ladies the other day, that I had often wondered why young women should marry, as they have so much more freedom, and so much more attention paid to them while unmarried. . . . I indeed did not mention the *strong* reason for their marrying—the *mechanical* reason." That *was* a strong reason, Boswell admitted; but did not imagination make it much more important than it was in reality? Was it not to a certain degree a delusion in men as well as in women. "Why yes, Sir; but it is a delusion that is always beginning again." "I don't know," mused Boswell, "but there is upon the whole more misery than happiness produced by that passion." "I don't think so, Sir."

Foiled when he approached the subject directly, Boswell tried an oblique attack with more success. Topham Beauclerk's wife, Lady Diana Beauclerk, who was consistently ill-treated by her husband, left him for another man. As Johnson tried to think highly of Beauclerk, his marriage was not a subject he would wish to discuss; and as Lady Diana was beautiful, the thought of her leaving Beauclerk's arms for another man's would increase his desire to avoid the subject. Boswell, therefore, opened out one day with a warm apology for Lady Diana, laying especial stress on her being still in the prime of life, "with qualities to produce happiness." At last Johnson could bear it no longer: "My dear Sir, never accustom your mind to mingle virtue and vice. The woman's a whore, and there's an end on't."

This dialogue was published during Lady Diana's life, and though Boswell suppressed her name he made it clear who was meant.

Another hit may be credited to Boswell, if the adornment of the male person is allowed to derive from the desire to charm the other sex. The subject of fine clothes having been introduced by Boswell, Johnson said that they were good only as they supplied the want of other means of procuring respect. Was Charles the Twelfth less respected for his coarse blue coat and black stock? And the King of Prussia dressed plain because the dignity of his character was sufficient.

"I here," says Boswell, "brought myself into a scrape, for I heedlessly said, 'Would not you, Sir, be the better for velvet and embroidery?' Johnson: 'Sir, you put an end to all argument when you introduce your opponent himself. Have you no better manners? There is *your* want.' I apologized by saying I had mentioned him as an instance of one who wanted as little as any man in the world, and yet, perhaps, might receive some additional lustre from dress."

(3)

The occasions when Boswell provoked Johnson unintentionally were quite as numerous as his intentional provocations. His worship of Johnson was as constant as any of his emotions could be, and made him relentless in his demands to be edified and instructed. Mixed with his worship was the desire to accumulate material for the Life, and the double pressure was often too much for Johnson. "I have been put so to the question by Bozzy, this morning," Johnson once complained to Mrs. Thrale, "that I am now panting for breath." Mrs. Thrale pressed for details. "Why," Johnson replied, "one question was: 'Pray, Sir, can you tell me why an apple is round and a pear pointed?' Would not such talk make a man hang himself?"

Plagued in this fashion, Johnson used to round on Boswell, and though Boswell's dramatic sense would make him record the punishment, his self-respect usually concealed the victim, whom he would refer to as a gentleman, as in the following episode. "He sometimes could not bear being teased with questions. I was present once when a gentleman asked so many as, 'What did you do, Sir?' 'What did you say, Sir?' that he at last grew enraged, and said, 'I will not be put to the question. Don't you consider, Sir, that these are not the manners of a gentleman? I will not be baited with what, and why; what is this? what is that? why is a cow's tail long? why is a fox's tail bushy?' The gentleman, who was a good deal out of countenance, said, 'Why, Sir, you are so good that I venture to trouble you.' Johnson: 'Sir, my being so good is no reason why you should be so ill.' "

Boswell's importunity and his prostration before Johnson

are both illustrated in a scene recorded by Fanny Burney.
Miss Burney, shortly after her great success with her first
novel, *Evelina,* was on a visit to the Thrales, and Boswell, who
had not read *Evelina,* was present.

Boswell's tone and manner, Miss Burney says, had an odd
mock solemnity, in unconscious imitation of Dr. Johnson;
and there was something slouching in his gait and dress as
though he had modelled himself on Dr. Johnson here, too.
His clothes were always too large for him; his hair, or wig,
was constantly in a state of negligence; and he never for a
moment sat still or upright upon a chair. Every look and
movement displayed either intentional or involuntary imitation. Yet certainly, she says, it was not meant as caricature,
for his heart, almost even to idolatry, was in his reverence of
Dr. Johnson. In the company of the Doctor, she continues,
Boswell seldom answered anything that was said, or attended
to anything that went forward, lest he should miss the smallest
sound from Dr. Johnson's voice, which when it burst forth
excited in him an attention that amounted almost to pain.
"His eyes goggled with eagerness; he leant his ear almost on
the shoulder of the Doctor; and his mouth dropped open to
catch every syllable that might be uttered; nay, he seemed not
only to dread losing a word, but to be anxious not to miss
a breathing, as if hoping from it, latently or mystically, some
information."

On the occasion described by Miss Burney, the company
was about to sit down to a meal, and Boswell made for the
seat next to Johnson, which was reserved for Miss Burney, to
whom Johnson was much attached. One of the guests told
Boswell that the place was Miss Burney's, at which Boswell
looked round with an important air as though demanding an

explanation. No explanation being vouchsafed, he took another chair, reluctantly and resentfully, and seated himself just behind Dr. Johnson, where he escaped observation for some time, until a sudden movement betrayed him. Turning angrily round, Johnson clapped his knee, and roared, "What do you there, Sir? Go to the table, Sir!" Boswell at once obeyed, but rose a little later to fetch something he wished to show Johnson. "What are you thinking of, Sir?" Johnson bellowed. "Why do you get up before the cloth is removed? Come back to your place, Sir! . . . Running about in the middle of meals! One would take you for a Branghton" (a family in *Evelina*).

"A Branghton, Sir? What is a Branghton, Sir?"

Johnson began to laugh. "Where have you lived, Sir," he asked, "and what company have you kept, not to know that?"

Boswell, who had crept back to his place, said nothing, but was presently heard by Fanny Burney to whisper to Mrs. Thrale: "Pray, Ma'am, what's a Branghton? Do me the favour to tell me! Is it some animal hereabouts?" Mrs. Thrale laughed and said nothing.

This high pressure of attentiveness and deference inevitably eased off on occasion, and when it did Johnson was more provoked than ever. Two of the most amusing scenes in Boswell record lapses of this kind.

One evening, on their Scotch tour, when they were riding through the Highlands, Johnson was tired and silent, and Boswell bored and possibly thirsty. As Johnson was attended by three guides, one leading his horse, one walking by his side, and one following in the rear, and as he was sunk in deep meditation, Boswell fancied the moment opportune to push on to the inn for which they were making. He thought, he says, there could be no harm in leaving Johnson for a little while. A roar from Johnson advised him of his mistake, and riding back he began to explain that he was anxious to see to Johnson's comfort at the inn, and to arrange for a boat to take them to Skye the next morning. Johnson cut him short with—"Do you know, I should as soon have thought of picking a pocket, as doing so?" "I am diverted with you, Sir," quavered Boswell. "Sir," Johnson bellowed, "I could never be diverted with incivility. Doing such a thing makes one lose confidence in him who has done it, as one cannot tell what he may do next." Though conscious, Boswell says, that his intentions were not improper, he was so confounded by Johnson's extraordinary warmth that he justified himself but lamely, and fell in again by Johnson's side.

Boswell's next lapse was even more heavily punished. They had reached the Isle of Skye, and were being entertained at Dunvegan by the Laird of Macleod. After dinner, when the ladies had retired, Johnson began to talk on animal and vegetable substances. Wool, he said, was an animal substance, and as flannel was made of wool it was less cleanly than linen. "I have often thought," he mused aloud, "that, if I kept a seraglio, the ladies should all wear linen gowns, or cotton—I mean stuffs made of vegetable substances. I would have no silk; you cannot tell when it is clean: It will be very nasty before it is perceived to be so."

"To hear the grave Dr. Samuel Johnson," Boswell writes, "that majestick teacher of moral and religious wisdom, while sitting solemn in an arm-chair in the Isle of Skye, talk, *ex cathedra*, of his keeping a seraglio, and acknowledge that the supposition had *often* been in his thoughts, struck me so forcibly with ludicrous contrast, that I could not but laugh immoderately. He was too proud to submit, even for a moment, to be the object of ridicule, and instantly retaliated with such keen, sarcastick wit, and such a variety of degrading images, of every one of which I was the object, that, though I can bear such attacks as well as most men, I yet found myself so much the sport of all the company, that I would gladly expunge from my mind every trace of this severe retort."

(4)

The outbursts provoked by Boswell, intentionally or unintentionally, are so vividly recorded that they tend to take up too much room in one's memory. In the greater number of the scenes he reproduces, he is an unobtrusive spectator who realizes that an interruption would spoil the effect; and when the scene is set by his own hand, as in the meeting of Wilkes and Johnson, he is especially careful to keep in the background. Yet even when he remained in the background, the scene often owed some of its life to him, for his mere presence, when he was not making a nuisance of himself, enlivened Johnson. Boswell, he once said, was the best travelling companion in the world, and in a letter to Mrs. Thrale he praised Boswell's good-humour and perpetual cheerfulness. The quality in him which appealed most to Johnson's repressed nature was his endless delight in the spectacle of life. Boswell writes somewhere of a walk he took through Derby, and the passage explains his attraction for Johnson. "I felt a pleasure in walking about Derby such as I always have in walking about any town to which I am not accustomed. There is an immediate sensation of novelty; and one speculates on the way in which life is passed in it, which, although there is a sameness everywhere upon the whole, is yet minutely diversified. The minute diversities in everything are wonderful."

To distinguish between the scenes in which Johnson was unconscious of Boswell's watchful eye and those in which it steadied or stimulated him is not always possible. In the following scene, for example, one cannot tell whether he remembered he had an audience. Johnson had secured a job for a small boy with Mr. Strahan, the printer. Having borrowed five guineas on account from Mr. Strahan, Johnson asked him to summon the boy, that he might give him one of the guineas. Boswell followed Johnson to the court-yard behind Mr. Strahan's house, and taking up a convenient position watched Johnson and the boy out of the corner of his eye. It was Johnson's practice to address everyone alike. He always, he said, spoke as intelligibly as he could.

"Well, my boy, how do you go on?"

"Pretty well, Sir," the urchin piped. "But they are afraid I an't strong enough for some parts of the business."

"Why, I shall be sorry for it; for when you consider with how little mental power and corporeal labour a printer can get a guinea a week, it is a very desirable occupation. Do you hear, take all the pains you can; and if this does not do, we must think of some other way of life for you. There's a guinea for you."

While paying a tribute to Johnson's active benevolence, Boswell adds that the slow and sonorous solemnity with which, while he bent himself down, he addressed a little, thick, short-legged boy, contrasted with the boy's awkwardness and awe, could not but excite some ludicrous emotions.

On the famous occasion when Boswell trapped Johnson

into meeting Wilkes, whom Johnson detested on political, moral, and religious grounds, Boswell both from prudence and artistic motives remained as unobtrusive as the smallness of the party allowed; keeping himself, in his own words, snug and silent, until Wilkes had melted Johnson's hostility. "No man," Boswell writes, "eat more heartily than Johnson, or loved better what was nice and delicate. Mr. Wilkes was very assiduous in helping him to some fine veal. 'Pray give me leave, Sir—It is better here—A little of the brown—Some fat, Sir—A little of the stuffing—Some gravy—Let me have the pleasure of giving you some butter—Allow me to recommend a squeeze of this orange; or the lemon, perhaps, may have more zest.' 'Sir, Sir, I am obliged to you, Sir,' cried Johnson, bowing, and turning his head to him with a look for some time of 'surly virtue,' but, in a short while, of complacency."

The awe which Johnson inspired in his company is a theme which Boswell, as Johnson's biographer, took a vicarious pride in, and when he gives examples of it, he remains as modestly in the background in his narrative as he remained in reality. Once, he relates, a large and distinguished company, who before Johnson's arrival had been freely discussing his merits and limitations, fell silent as he entered the room. "We were all," says Boswell, "as quiet as a school upon the entrance of the headmaster." On another occasion Johnson set everyone, except the Bishop of Killaloe, tittering by the gravity with which he praised a certain woman as having a "bottom of good sense." "Where's the merriment?" he demanded, glancing sternly round, and then very slowly pronouncing, as though he challenged anyone to laugh, "I say the woman was fundamentally sensible." "We all sat composed as at a funeral," Boswell adds.

Boswell's willingness to sacrifice his own vanity in order to bring out some aspect of Johnson, the rarest of biographical gifts, has been used by many critics as proof of his contemptible character. "Everything which another man would have hidden," Macaulay says, "everything which would have made another man hang himself, was matter of gay and clamorous exultation to his weak and diseased mind." In support of this denunciation, Macaulay adduces among other instances one of the finest scenes in Boswell. During a storm at sea in the Hebrides, Boswell became terrified, and to keep him quiet the pilot gave him a rope to pull. The rope was fixed to the top of one of the masts, and if he had considered the matter, Boswell says, he would have seen that to pull at the rope could not be of any service. But the pilot's object, as he realized later, was to keep him out of the way of those who were working the vessel. Johnson meanwhile was lying in a bunk, a greyhound at his back to keep him warm, and was discovered in philosophic tranquillity by Boswell, when the ship at last reached harbour.

Boswell would have appeared to better advantage had he written: "Dr. Johnson, wisely perhaps, elected to go below as the storm became really violent, but I was unwilling to miss so novel an experience, and insisted on remaining on deck, I fear at some inconvenience to the gallant fellows who were forcing the vessel through dangers which threatened at each moment to engulf her." But he realized that Johnson's calm was made more vivid by the contrast with his own panic. That the sacrifice of his vanity was deliberate appears from a note to another scene. One evening in the Isle of Skye, when Johnson had gone to bed, Boswell was prevailed upon to drink with his host. After the second bowl he was well warmed, after the third he was cordial and merry to a high degree, and after the fourth he lost all distinct recollection of the proceedings. On the following day, awaking with a severe headache, he was angry with himself, and felt his conduct had been very inconsistent with what he ought to maintain as the companion of the Rambler. At one Johnson looked in on him. "What, drunk yet?" he asked, but in a friendly tone which abated Boswell's anxiety. They had kept him up, he pleaded. "No, you kept them up, you drunken dog," Johnson replied, with a smile which encouraged Boswell to get out of bed and go in search of some brandy, a draught of which dispelled his headache.

In the note to this scene Boswell answers the many critics of his ingenuous candour on this and other occasions. "Here, as in every other part of the present work," he writes, "my principal object was to delineate Dr. Johnson's manners and character. In justice to him I would not omit an anecdote, which, though in some degree to my own disadvantage, exhibits in so strong a light the indulgence and good-humour with which he could treat those excesses in his friends, of which he highly disapproved." In other instances, too, Boswell adds, the critics had misunderstood his motive for recording particulars, the objections to which he saw as clearly as they.

(5)

That Boswell was not always ingenuously candid in his portrait of Johnson has been shown in the examples given of his practice of pricking Johnson, and then recording the roar with puzzled wonder. His other failures to be entirely honest must now be considered.

The most debatable of these is his treatment of Goldsmith, which has been singled out for harsher criticism than it deserves. The fact that his sketch of Goldsmith's person and character is a fairly exact likeness of Boswell suggests rather an unconscious antipathy to someone who made him more aware of his own defects than a deliberate caricature. Nor is there any reason to suppose that his slighting references to Goldsmith's work hid a high appreciation of its merits. Even Johnson, though he said that Goldsmith was a very great man and that he touched nothing which he did not adorn, dismissed *The Vicar of Wakefield* as a mere fanciful performance. To Goldsmith's contemporaries his weaknesses as a man obscured his genius. As his merits were more fully appreciated, and new generations arose to whom he was known only as a writer, Boswell's attitude to him seemed increasingly malicious, until at last Boswell was transformed into an envious Scot who tried to embroil a great-hearted Englishman and a warm-hearted Irishman.

That Boswell made mischief between Johnson and Goldsmith may be taken for granted. It is probable, too, that he picked Goldsmith out for special treatment, for Goldsmith was his most serious rival as Johnson's future biographer. Although as early as the spring of 1773 Boswell announced, and Johnson approved, his intention to write Johnson's life, no one foresaw what an achievement it would be. It was certain that there would be several attempts, and it was assumed that if Goldsmith wrote on Johnson, any other life would be negligible in comparison. Goldsmith's death set Boswell's mind at rest, and the patronizing tone he adopts towards Goldsmith expresses rather his tolerance of someone he fears no longer than the settled malice which has been discerned in it. If one compares Boswell's account of Johnson and Goldsmith with Mrs. Thrale's and Miss Reynolds's, Goldsmith is found to come off much better with Boswell than with the two ladies, though neither disliked him.

"The dog," Johnson said to Mrs. Thrale, who was discussing Goldsmith as his future biographer, "would write it best, to be sure, but his particular malice towards me, and general disregard for truth, would make the book useless to all, and injurious to my character."

Dr. Johnson, Miss Reynolds writes, appeared to have much more kindness for Goldsmith than Goldsmith had for him. Goldsmith always seemed to be overawed by him, particularly when in company with people of any consequence, as if impressed with fear of disgrace.

Boswell gives several examples of Goldsmith's mortification at Johnson's conversational supremacy. He illustrates, too, his childish vanity, which sprung from his constant sense of his own unimpressiveness. Johnson used to abbreviate the names of his friends—Lanky for Langton, Bozzy for Boswell, and so on. "We are all in labour for a name to Goldy's play," he once said; and Goldsmith exclaimed, "I have often desired him not to call me Goldy." But Boswell also shows Goldsmith at ease with Johnson and even scoring off him. The art of writing a good fable, he said to Reynolds one day, consisted in maintaining a simple style. In the fable of the little fishes who petitioned Jupiter to be changed into birds, the skill lay in making them talk like little fishes. Johnson began to shake with laughter. "Why, Dr. Johnson," Goldsmith retorted, "this is not as easy as you seem to think; for if you were to make little fishes talk, they would talk like WHALES." Another day, Johnson having pooh-poohed a project of Goldsmith's for a theatre which should exhibit only new plays, Goldsmith said, "Ay, ay, this may be nothing to you, who can now shelter yourself behind the corner of a pension"; and Johnson accepted the reproof.

It is to Boswell, too, that we owe the preservation of Goldsmith's famous, "Johnson, to be sure, has a roughness of manner; but no man alive has a more tender heart. He has nothing of the bear but his skin."

Very different is Boswell's treatment of his two rival biographers, Mrs. Thrale and Sir John Hawkins.

While Johnson was alive, Boswell and Mrs. Thrale were ostensibly on good terms. The immense material which Mrs. Thrale could give him about Johnson, if he could coax it out of her, dangled temptingly before Boswell's eyes, and as late as the summer of 1782, two years before Johnson's death, Boswell was writing to her almost like a lover: "Last night's post brought me your kind letter informing me of Dr. Johnson's being so much better since his jaunt to Oxford. It is needless to tell you what joy it gave me. I kissed the subscription, H. L. Thrale, with fervency. . . . My dear Madam, from the day that I first had the pleasure to meet you, when I jumpt into your coach, not, I hope, from impudence, but from that agreeable kind of attraction which makes one forget ceremony, I have invariably thought of you with admiration and gratitude." The letter ends with the suggestion that as Mrs. Thrale writes so easily, she might by a small expense of time give him much pleasure with anecdotes of their gay and literary friends, and particularly of the illustrious Imlac (Johnson).

Mrs. Thrale's failure to hand over the material which she

wished to use herself, and which she had collected at such expense to her comfort, produced a drastic change in Boswell's attitude. The chief omission in the later portion of Boswell's Life is a full account of Johnson's relations with the Thrales, and of the quarrel over Piozzi. Boswell resented this omission. If, he says, Mrs. Thrale would publish the whole of the correspondence between herself and Dr. Johnson concerning her marriage with Piozzi, a full view of his sentiments would be available. Until then, he adds, the world must content itself with Johnson's remark to Sir John Hawkins: "Poor Thrale! I thought that either her virtue or her vice would have restrained her from such a marriage. She is now become a subject for her enemies to exult over; and for her friends, if she has any left, to forget, or pity."

If we bear in mind the resentment of the baffled Boswell, which was further sharpened by his jealousy of a rival biographer, we shall liberally discount his criticisms of Mrs. Thrale's anecdotes. Mrs. Thrale was flighty and scatter-brained. When she relied on her memory, instead of on her common-place book, she mixed her dates and muddled the talk she recorded, and her feeling towards Johnson was in some degree warped by his attitude to her marriage with Piozzi. But, after all deductions, she shows a Johnson who is more human than Boswell's though less entertaining. With her he was a man, with Boswell he was a character. He confided to her many details of his life which he withheld from everyone else; and even his sayings, thanks to her common-place book, are often caught by her with a skill not much below Boswell's.

The pages of analysis to which Boswell subjects the "Anecdotes," which he dismisses at the end with "perhaps I may be thought to have dwelt too long upon her little collection," set the fashion, which still flourishes, of underrating an invaluable contribution to our knowledge of Johnson. That Boswell's analysis was not only coloured by jealousy and resentment, but deliberately dishonest, is shown when he corrects one of Mrs. Thrale's stories on the authority of Baretti. Baretti, who was tutor to Thrale's children, hated Mrs. Thrale; his insane temper made him assert and believe the most absurd fictions about those he disliked, and he disliked nearly everyone, including Boswell, who returned his dislike so vigorously that when Baretti was on trial for his life, Boswell went about London expressing the hope that he would be hanged.

Boswell is equally unfair to Hawkins, whose life of Johnson he describes as a farrago, a very small part of which relates to the person who is the subject of the book. This is literally accurate, but Hawkins's work is so enormous that the part dealing with Johnson is only relatively small, and from this part Boswell took much of value without adequate acknowledgment, and omitted to take much else of value, probably from a fear that if his borrowings were exposed, the merits of his book would be denied, and the attention of the public diverted to Hawkins. Hawkins's account of the Ivy Lane Club in 1749, and his narrative of Johnson's last days, are, to give two instances, very inadequately drawn on by Boswell. "Sir John Hawkins, Knight," Boswell calls him, "a man whom, during my long intimacy with Dr. Johnson, I never saw in his company—I think but once, and I am sure not above twice." This remark cuts both ways, and might equally well have appeared in Hawkins's Life, with Boswell substituted for Hawkins. Hawkins knew Johnson for nearly forty years; he was chosen by Johnson as one of his executors, and probably spent many more hours in Johnson's company than Boswell, in spite of the three months' tour in Scotland.

When her father's life of Johnson appeared, Miss Laetitia Hawkins narrates, Boswell showed himself very uneasy under an injury which he was much embarrassed to define. Sir John, referring to the Scottish tour, had spoken of him as "Mr. James Boswell, a native of Scotland," and Boswell called on Sir John to express his vexation. "Well, but, *Mr. James Boswell!*" he kept on articulating. "Surely, surely, *Mr. James Boswell!*" "I know what you mean," Sir John at last interrupted; "you would have had me say that Johnson undertook this tour with The Boswell."

Though relevant to nothing except a study of Miss Laetitia Hawkins, her defence of Johnson's piety must be inserted here, for its own unique sake. "Much has been written regarding Johnson's excessive, nay, superstitious scrupulousness, but in my opinion without considering his infirmities. Had he realized that the service required by the Gospel is perfect freedom, he would have abandoned efforts at self-perfection and lived at ease. Such was not to be, and his persistence is the more laudable because it was not stimulated by the use of wine or drugs."

To return to Boswell. There are many lesser instances of misrepresentation scattered through the Life. If our knowledge of his relations with his contemporaries were complete, we might have to discount his accuracy on scores of occasions; but even such knowledge as we possess is enough to put us on our guard where certain persons are concerned. Bishop

Percy, for example, annoyed Boswell both by the fewness of
the anecdotes he sent Boswell for the Life and by his request
that his name should not be mentioned. "As to suppressing
your Lordship's name," Boswell replied, "when relating the
very few anecdotes of Johnson with which you have favoured
me, I will do anything to oblige you but that very thing. I
owe it to the authenticity of my work, to its respectability,
and to the credit of my illustrious friend, to introduce as
many names of eminent persons as I can. . . . Believe me,
my Lord, you are not the only bishop in the number of great
men with which my pages are graced. I am quite resolute as
to this matter." In the light of this letter, one cannot but
wonder if Boswell reported with complete impartiality the
scene in which Percy first put up a very disingenuous defence
of a Dr. Mounsey against the charge of swearing and talking
bawdy, and then, when Johnson exposed his disingenuousness, left the room in a temper. Even if the scene is correctly
reported, as it may be, for Percy was inclined to gloss over
anything that hurt his sense of decorum, it illustrates Boswell's maliciousness, a quality in him which struck his contemporaries more forcibly than it strikes us. "How many
maggots have crawled out of that great body!" Burke exclaimed when he read the Life, which contains many flattering passages about him, but also discloses that Johnson
doubted his honesty as a politician, deplored his attempts at
humour, and believed he would not hesitate to go with a
prostitute.

Burke and Percy were too well known, and too important,
to be seriously misrepresented by Boswell, who was doubtless
quite satisfied with the digs he gave them; and they even
gain in reality from the dash of malice with which he treats

them. But in dealing with lesser persons, Boswell sometimes suppresses the truth or completely distorts it. Johnson during the last weeks of his life was constantly visited by a teacher of Italian, called Sastres. "The good Mr. Hoole," Fanny Burney writes, "and the equally good Mr. Sastres attend Dr. Johnson rather as nurses than as friends, for they sit whole hours by him without even speaking to him." Johnson wrote several letters to Sastres, and because Sastres would not hand them over to Boswell, Boswell says nothing of his attendance on the dying Johnson, and mentions him only to illustrate the diversity of Johnson's acquaintance. Johnson, he says, was at once the companion of the brilliant Colonel Forester of the Guards and of the awkward and uncouth Robert Levett; of Lord Thurlow and Mr. Sastres, the Italian master.

Boswell's account of his and Johnson's cavalier treatment of Sir John Dalrymple provides a more complex example of the misrepresentation he indulges in when his malice is aroused. Towards the close of their Scottish tour, Johnson and Boswell were invited to stay the night with Sir John Dalrymple. Sir John, Boswell says, had expressed astonishment that any Scottish gentleman could keep company with Johnson; and Boswell accordingly resolved, though he does not say so, to make Sir John suffer. By various devices he delayed Johnson on the way to Sir John, and at the dinner-hour they were still several miles from Sir John's house. Johnson, says Boswell, who knew Sir John and his friends would read his account of the tour, did not seem much troubled at the baronet being treated with so little attention to politeness, and became jocular when Boswell talked of the grievous disappointment Sir John, who had killed a seven-year-old sheep in their honour, would feel when they did not arrive for the feast. Sir John was an historian, and Johnson amused himself as they drove along with a parody of Sir John's style. "Dinner being ready," said Johnson, laughing heartily, "he wondered that his guests were not yet come. His wonder was soon succeeded by impatience. He walked about the room in anxious agitation; sometimes he looked at his watch, sometimes he looked out of the window with an eager gaze of expectation, and revolved in his mind the various accidents of human life. . . . The mind of man can bear a certain pressure; but there is a point where it can bear no more. A rope was in his view, and he died a Roman death."

That Johnson, punctiliously polite except in the heat of talk, deliberately lingered on the way to Sir John, and was content to arrive some hours after dinner, is an obvious invention. All the details of the tour were left to Boswell. Johnson knew nothing of the distances to be covered, and the moment when he realized that they would be late, with its accompanying explosion, has clearly been suppressed by Boswell, who gives only the humorous extravagances with which Johnson, after he had gored Boswell sufficiently, allayed his uneasiness at what was on his part an unintentional discourtesy.

Boswell has here sacrificed Johnson to satisfy his own malice. In the most thorough of all his misrepresentations he sacrifices the truth in order not to weaken his picture of Johnson as the invincible despot of every company.

One day at Mr. Dilly's, Boswell was present at an argument between Johnson and Mrs. Knowles, a famous Quakeress. The subject of dispute was a young girl, Miss Harry, whom Johnson had been very fond of. Miss Harry had been converted to Quakerism by Mrs. Knowles, to the anger both of Johnson and her father, who cut her out of his will, from which she would have received one hundred thousand pounds.

Anna Seward was present during the argument, and she wrote a full account of it directly afterwards, and sent it some years later to Boswell, at his request. Her account is of the highest interest for several reasons. A comparison of it with Boswell's travestied version illustrates his unscrupulousness; it is the fullest extant specimen of a dialogue between Johnson and another person; and it shows how impossible it was to dislodge Johnson by reasoning from a position which he chose to defend with his inexhaustible powers of retort.

"Mrs. K.: I am to ask thy indulgence, Doctor, towards a gentle female to whom thou usedst to be kind, and who is uneasy in the loss of that kindness. Jenny Harry weeps at the consciousness that thou wilt not speak to her.

"Dr. J.: Madam, I hate the odious wench, and desire you will not talk to me about her.

"Mrs. K.: Yet what is her crime, Doctor?

"Dr. J.: Apostasy, Madam; apostasy from the community in which she was educated.

"Mrs. K.: Surely the quitting one community for another cannot be a crime, if it is done from motives of conscience. Hadst thou been educated in the Romish Church, I must suppose thou wouldst have abjured its errors, and that there would have been merit in the abjuration.

"Dr. J.: Madam, if I had been educated in the Roman

Catholic faith, I believe I should have questioned my right to quit the religion of my fathers; therefore, well may I hate the arrogance of a young wench, who sets herself up for a judge on theological points, and deserts the religion in whose bosom she was nurtured.

"Mrs. K.: She has not done so; the name and the faith of Christians are not denied to the sectaries.

"Dr. J.: If the name is not, the common sense is.

"Mrs. K.: I will not dispute this point with thee, Doctor, at least at present; it would carry us too far. Suppose it granted that, in the mind of a young girl, the weaker arguments appeared the strongest, her want of judgment should excite thy pity, not thy resentment.

"Dr. J.: Madam, it has my anger and my contempt, and always will have them.

"Mrs. K.: Consider, Doctor, she must be *sincere*. Consider what a noble fortune she has sacrificed.

"Dr. J.: Madam, Madam, I have never taught myself to consider that the association of folly can extenuate guilt.

"Mrs. K.: Ah! Doctor, we cannot rationally suppose that the Deity will not pardon a defect in judgment (supposing it should prove one) in that breast where the consideration of serving him, according to its idea, in spirit and truth, has been a preferable inducement to that of worldly interest.

"Dr. J.: Madam, I pretend not to set bounds to the mercy of the Deity; but I hate the wench, and shall ever hate her. I hate all impudence; but the impudence of a chit's apostasy I *nauseate*.

"Mrs. K.: Jenny is a very gentle creature. She trembles to have offended her parent, though far removed from his presence; she grieves to have offended her guardian, and she is sorry to have offended Dr. Johnson, whom she loved, admired, and honoured.

"Dr. J.: Why, then, Madam, did she not consult the man whom she pretends to have loved, admired, and honoured, upon her new-fangled scruples? If she had looked up to that man with any degree of the respect she professes, she would have supposed his ability to judge of fit and right, at least equal to that of a raw wench just out of her primer.

"Mrs. K.: Ah! Doctor, remember it was not amongst the witty and the learned that Christ selected his disciples, and constituted the teachers of his precepts. Jenny thinks Dr. Johnson great and good; but she also thinks the gospel demands and enjoins a simpler form of worship than that of the established church; and that it is not in wit and eloquence to supersede the force of what appears to her a plain and regular system, which cancels all typical and mysterious ceremonies, as fruitless and even idolatrous; and asks only obedience to its injunctions, and the ingenuous homage of a devout heart.

"Dr. J.: The homage of a fool's head, Madam, you should say, if you will pester me about the ridiculous wench.

"Mrs. K.: If thou choosest to suppose her ridiculous, thou canst not deny that she has been religious, sincere, disinterested. Canst thou believe that the gate of Heaven will be shut to the tender and pious mind, whose *first* consideration has been that of apprehended duty?

"Dr. J.: Pho, pho, Madam; who says it will?

"Mrs. K.: Then if Heaven shuts not its gate, shall man shut his heart? If the Deity accept the homage of such as sincerely serve him under every form of worship, Dr. Johnson and this humble girl will, it is to be hoped, meet in a blessed eternity, whither human animosity must *not* be carried.

"Dr. J.: Madam, I am not fond of meeting fools anywhere; they are detestable company, and while it is in my power to avoid conversing with them, I certainly shall exert that power; and so you may tell the odious wench, whom you have persuaded to think herself a saint, and of whom you will, I suppose, make a preacher; but I shall take care she does not preach to *me*."

At this final bellow, Miss Seward records, Boswell whispered to her: "I never saw this mighty lion so chafed before." Miss Harry's renunciation of a great fortune enraged Johnson both as a reproach to his own comparative lethargy as a follower of Christ, and as an insult to the sceptical element in him, which rose in disgust against the idea of paying one hundred thousand pounds for the privilege of worshipping Christ in one way rather than another. He was also exasperated by Mrs. Knowles's disparagement of the Roman Catholic Church, to which his desire for protection against his terrors inclined him, and which he once said he would have joined but for "an obstinate rationality." There was nothing for it but to roar his way out of this entanglement, if he could, but at every rush he was pricked back by the lance of his mild and dauntless opponent, and though he would not yield, he could not escape.

Boswell was quite aware of Johnson's discomfiture. It is true that he had turned up at the dinner in "high spirits," which he attributed to a talk with Mr. Orme, the weighty and erudite historian of British India. But his faculties were not so clouded as to miss the general effect of what passed; and he commented later to Miss Seward on the ferocious, reasonless, and unchristian violence of Johnson.

After Miss Seward had sent her account to Boswell, she wrote to Mrs. Knowles that she feared Boswell would shrink from inserting it in his life of the Colossus. Her fears were well grounded. There is no reference in Boswell to Miss Seward's report, and he dismisses an account sent him by Mrs. Knowles, at his request, in these terms: "As I had not the least recollection of it, and did not find the smallest trace of it in my Record taken at the time, I could not in consistency with my firm regard to authenticity, insert it in my work. . . . It chiefly relates to the principles of the sect called Quakers; and no doubt the Lady appears to have greatly the advantage of Dr. Johnson in argument as well as expression."

Mrs. Knowles's account is in general agreement with Miss Seward's, though as it was written much later it is less detailed. Boswell's version contains no reference to Quakerism, in spite of Miss Harry's conversion to that form of worship being the subject in dispute; it allows Mrs. Knowles three short sentences, totalling twenty words in all, in defence of her creed and of the girl she had converted; and it shows Johnson, after dismissing Miss Harry as an odious wench, in full possession of the argument, which he develops at a level by no means too high for Boswell to climb to without any assistance from his recollection, if any, of what Johnson actually said.

CHAPTER SEVEN

Benevolence, Real and Fictitious—Travels—
The Lives of the Poets

(1)

MONEY for travel, and unlimited leisure to talk, were
the two chief advantages the pension brought to
Johnson. When he was in London, whether he was in bed
or sitting over his tea, his mornings were spent in conversing
with his many visitors. He seemed, a friend said, to be considered a kind of public oracle whom everyone thought they
had a right to consult. The midday meal at a tavern, and
tea and supper at some friend's house, gave further opportunities for talk, and he rarely returned home till late.

Macaulay has stamped on the popular imagination the
idea that the Literary Club, which was founded in 1764, was
the great arena of Johnson's conversational triumphs, an
arena nightly strewn with famous victims. But though his
pre-eminence in a society which included Burke, Reynolds,
Gibbon, and Fox must have pleased him, the records of the
club show that after the first few years he seldom attended.
The comforts of Streatham attracted him more strongly, and
when he was in town he preferred to be with friends, at whose
houses he knew what society he would meet, rather than go
to the club, which as it extended its membership included
many persons he did not like. In an estimate of Johnson as
a talker, his evenings at the club, which are very scantily reported by Boswell, have no special place.

His most obvious characteristic as a talker, his determination not to yield the victory to his opponent, was what impressed his hearers most, and their record of his talk therefore reveals what was most striking in him rather than what was most profound and sincere. Having no power over others except what his wits and force gave him, he could satisfy his desire for domination only in talk. He thought it necessary, Reynolds says, never to be worsted in an argument, and Boswell complains that when Johnson perceived his opponent to be gaining ground, he had recourse to some robust mode of sophistry. "Once when I was pressing upon him with visible advantage," Boswell says, "he stopped me thus:—'My dear Boswell, let's have no more of this; you'll make nothing of it. I'd rather have you whistle a Scottish tune.' " Talk being his field of battle, he approached it fully armed, and with the weak points of the enemy all present to his mind, as appears incidentally in his praise of Reynolds, whom he called the most invulnerable man he knew, the man whom, if he should quarrel with him, he would find the most difficult to abuse.

His claim that no man was so cautious as himself not to interrupt others, or thought it so necessary to appear attentive when others were speaking, is an extreme instance of a great talker being so much impressed by his occasional silences as to be altogether deceived about both their length and frequency. Once when Johnson was praising Burke's talk, Boswell interjected that Burke could listen, too. Johnson would not have this, and his answer shows that he expected complete silence from the company whenever he was speaking. "So desirous is Burke to talk, that, if one is speaking at this end of the table, he'll speak to somebody at the other end."

One evening, when Langton was present, Burke started topic after topic, but before he could begin to develop them, Johnson made them his own. As Langton and Burke were walking away, Burke praised the brilliance Johnson had shown. Langton agreed, but added he could have wished to hear more from Burke. "Oh, no," Burke answered, "it is enough for me to have rung the bell to him."

Such talks as these have not been recorded by Boswell, but their nature can be guessed from what is finest in Johnson's writing. What his writing does not illustrate is the range of his wit. In his milder moments it was often pictorial and imaginative. Boswell one day was defending suicide as the last refuge of a detected swindler. "Let him go abroad to a distant country," said Johnson; "let him go to some place where he is *not* known. Don't let him go to the Devil where he *is* known." The most famous of his triumphs in this style is his reply to the Scotsman who claimed that Scotland had a great many noble, wild prospects. "I believe you, Sir, you have a great many. Norway, too, has noble, wild prospects; and Lapland is remarkable for prodigious noble, wild prospects. But, Sir, let me tell you, the noblest prospect which a Scotsman ever sees is the high road that leads him to England!"

Direct attacks provoked sharper and simpler retorts. He was praising the Scotch scholar, Buchanan, when a Scot interrupted with: "Ah, Dr. Johnson, what would you have said of Buchanan had he been an Englishman?" "Why, Sir," Johnson replied, after a slight pause, "I should *not* have said of Buchanan, had he been an Englishman, what I will now say of him as a Scotsman—that he was the only man of genius his country ever produced." To another Scot, who reminded him that, after all, God had made Scotland, he replied that God had made it for Scotsmen, and that God had also made Hell. Equally final was his retort to the sister-in-law of a friend. Johnson disliked anyone who claimed to be happy, and the lady having made this claim in an emphatic voice, Johnson turned to his friend and said: "If your sister-in-law is indeed the contented being she professes herself, Sir, her life gives the lie to every research of humanity; for she is happy without health, without beauty, without money, and without understanding." He refused, when he narrated this incident to Mrs. Thrale, to admit any remorse. "I tell you," he roared, "the woman is ugly and sickly, and foolish and poor; and would it not make a man hang himself to hear such a creature say it was happy?" He was equally obdurate when the President of Jesus, Oxford, tried to be amusing at his expense. "Indeed, indeed, Doctor," cried the President, frightened by a tremendous snarl, "I meant nothing." "Sir, if you mean nothing, say nothing," answered Johnson, and was silent for the rest of the evening.

The rude vigour of his retorts has obscured the extenuating fact that he himself was always a sick man. In private he regretted the explosions of his overstrained nerves. "When I am musing alone," he wrote to Dr. Taylor, "I feel a pang for every moment that any human being has by my peevishness or obstinacy spent in uneasiness." He was always sorry, he once said, when he made bitter speeches, and never made them but when he was insufferably vexed.

If his victim was pert, like the lady whose happiness he questioned, and perhaps extinguished for ever, or feebly facetious, as the President of Jesus may have been, Johnson could not bring himself to express his compunction. But on many occasions, as his biographers have shown, he did everything he could to soothe the offended person.

Miss Reynolds narrates how the Dean of Derry was once browbeaten by Johnson for maintaining that no one improved after forty-five. "You, who perhaps are forty-eight," said Johnson, "may still improve if you will try; I wish you would set about it . . . there is great room for it." After dinner Johnson took Miss Reynolds aside, and said how sorry he was for the way he had spoken. "You very well may," Miss Reynolds reports herself as replying, and continues with the same indifference to grammar: "When the Dean came up into the Drawing-Room, Dr. Johnson immediately rose from his seat, and made him sit on the sophy by him, and with such a beseeching look of pardon, and with such fond gestures —literally smoothing down his arms and his knees—tokens of penitence, which were so graciously received by the Dean as to make Dr. Johnson very happy. . . ."

The Dean, though pacified at the moment, wrote some ironical verses on Johnson's politeness. Horace Walpole saw these verses and commented: "A properer answer would have been to fling a glass of wine in his face. I have no patience with an unfortunate monster trusting to his helpless deformity for indemnity for any impertinence that his arrogance suggests, and who thinks that what he has read is an excuse for everything he says." The Dean would not have endorsed these stout words from a person whom Johnson could have tossed out of the window without pausing in his talk. But his vexation remained active; he told Boswell that when Johnson smiled he showed the teeth at the corners of his mouth, and while admitting his immense respect for Johnson's brains dismissed him from the social standpoint with, "In short, he is not a gentleman."

So far as a gentleman is one who subordinates his personal feelings in the interests of social harmony, Johnson fell a long way short of being one. He understood the theory of good breeding, stating in *The Rambler* as the first law of politeness that "no man shall give any preference to himself." Nor was the gulf between theory and practice never bridged. At Lord Monboddo's, Boswell narrates, Johnson insisted on standing up as the ladies left the room after dinner, and then delivered a discourse on politeness, which he defined as "fictitious benevolence," and praised as supplying the absence of real affection between those who met only in public. But, as this incident suggests, politeness was not second nature to him. Even in his letters the clanking of the machinery is audible whenever he sets himself to the task of being merely courteous, though he could rise majestically to great occasions, as in the acknowledgment to Lord Bute of his pension: "Bounty always receives part of its value from the manner in which it is bestowed; your Lordship's kindness includes every circumstance that can gratify delicacy, or enforce obligation. You have conferred your favours on a man who has neither alliance nor interest, who has not merited them by services, nor courted them by officiousness; you have spared him the shame of solicitation, and the anxiety of suspense."

His most sustained achievement in "fictitious benevolence" was in his relations with Mrs. Boswell. Whether Mrs. Boswell regarded Johnson as the magnet which drew Boswell to London, or merely as a pretext for her husband's urgent journeys to a place which he somewhere calls "the great emporium for ladies of easy virtue," she disliked Johnson before they met, and did not like him better when she had to entertain him at Auchinleck. No man, says Boswell of the meeting between Johnson and Mrs. Boswell, could be more polite when he chose to be so, and his conversation soon charmed her into a forgetfulness of his external appearance. Johnson did not share Boswell's illusion, and in a letter he wrote Mrs. Boswell three years later said: "You will now have Mr. Boswell home; it is well that you have him; he has led a wild life. . . . Pray take care of him, and tame him. The only thing in which I have the honour to agree with you is, in loving him; and while we are so much of a mind in a matter of so much importance, our other quarrels will, I hope, produce no great bitterness." In the following year he wrote to Boswell that he was glad to hear his old enemy, Mrs. Boswell, was beginning to feel some remorse, and a few months later she sent him a jar of marmalade, which he acknowledged charmingly: "I received it as a token of friendship, as a proof of reconciliation, things much sweeter than sweetmeats. . . . By having your kindness I think I have a double security for the continuance of Mr. Boswell's, which it is not to be expected that any man can long keep, when the influence of a lady so highly and so justly valued operates against him. Mr. Boswell will tell you that I was always faithful to your interest, and always endeavoured to exalt you in his estimation."

Boswell may not have enjoyed, or even thought very gentlemanly, Johnson's suggestion that he needed looking after in his wife's absence; but as Mrs. Boswell and Johnson were henceforth on good terms, and she even invited him of her own accord to Auchinleck, Johnson's management of her must be allowed to show that he could exercise finesse in social matters. But that he was fundamentally indifferent to the gentleman's code of behaviour is plainly shown by the evidence he gave at Baretti's trial. As the gentleman is a product of wealth and security, he feels the need to counter-act the enervating effects of his environment, and therefore values courage as highly as good breeding. His ideal is com-plete self-possession, whether in the drawing-room or on the field of battle, and he ignores the possibility of cowardice either in himself or in his friends. Johnson, most of whose life was spent in poverty and insecurity, judged everyone as an individual, not as a member of a class; and though him-self exceptionally courageous, saw no reason to assume that his friends were equally so. His evidence on behalf of Baretti could not have been given by a gentleman. The Chevalier Bayard, for example, would have sent Baretti to the gallows rather than cast the faintest slur on his personal courage, and would have felt that in so doing he had discharged the ordinary obligations of friendship.

Three men had set on Baretti in the Haymarket. Baretti ran off, was pursued, and, turning to defend himself, stabbed one of his assailants. The man died, and Baretti was ar-raigned for murder at the Old Bailey. Tributes to his char-acter were offered by a number of eminent men, including Reynolds, Burke, Garrick, Goldsmith, and Johnson. Baretti, according to Reynolds, was a man of great humanity and very active in helping his friends. According to Burke, he was a thorough good-natured man; according to Garrick, the most actively benevolent man of his acquaintance; and ac-cording to Goldsmith, who had had a violent quarrel with him, most humane, benevolent, and peaceable. Johnson confined himself to the two points about which the court wished to be informed, whether Baretti was naturally combative and whether he was drunk at the time of the scuffle. "I have no reason," Johnson said, "to think he was ever disordered with liquor in his life. A man that I never knew to be otherwise than peaceable, and a man that I take to be rather timorous."

Real as distinguished from fictitious benevolence is not an essential attribute of a gentleman. He may possess it, but his regard for appearances makes him awkward in dealing with the reality of suffering. Johnson had none of this squeamishness. His charity to the poor has been illustrated. Of the many recorded instances of his help to those suffering from other evils than poverty, two may be given.

His friend Miss Reynolds fell out with her brother, for whom she had kept house during some years. Joshua Reynolds seems to have been too worldly for his sisters, one of whom wrote to him: "It may be, thy soul is past all recovery. If so, I shall never see thee more. Thy vissitation is not yet come: and who knows in what shape it will come: or whether it will come at all. Wo be to thee if it does not come." The Miss Reynolds whom Johnson knew was less forceful, but probably even more exasperating. She lived, Miss Burney says, in an habitual perplexity of mind and irresolution of conduct, which to herself was restlessly tormenting, and to all around her teasingly wearisome.

Having applied to Johnson for advice how to make it up with her brother, and enclosed for his remarks a letter she had written Joshua, Miss Reynolds received from Johnson a letter which he advised her to send instead of hers.

"DEAR BROTHER,—I know that complainers are never welcome, yet you must allow me to complain of your unkindness, because it lies heavy at my heart and because I am not conscious that I ever deserved it. I have not perhaps been always careful enough to please, but you can charge me, and I can charge myself with no offence which a Brother may not forgive.

"If you ask me what I suffer from you, I answer that I suffer too much in the loss of your notice; but to that is added the neglect of the world which is the consequence of yours.

"If you ask me what will satisfy me, I shall be satisfied with such a degree of attention when I visit you, as may set me above the contempt of your servants, with your calling now and then at my lodgings and your inviting me now and then with such parties as I may properly appear in. This is not much for a sister who has at least done you no harm, and this I hope you will promise by your answer to this letter; for a refusal will give me more pain than you can desire or intend to inflict."

It appears from an accompanying note that Johnson felt he had not quite caught Miss Reynolds's style, for, while telling her that he preferred his letter to the one she had submitted for his approval, he suggested that she should alter any expressions which she did not think ladylike.

Her alterations were not, hardly perhaps could have been, sufficient to conceal the real author from Reynolds. Reynolds passed the story on to Northcote, and Northcote improved on it by giving a still more Johnsonian ring to the first sentence: "I am well aware that complaints are always odious, but complain I must."

Other qualities as well as goodness of heart are illustrated by Johnson's attempt in 1777 to save Dr. Dodd from the gallows.

Dodd was at one time a fashionable preacher, and a favourite with society women. His sermons, as the clergyman celebrated by Max Beerbohm suggested to Johnson, were addressed to the passions. Alexander Carlyle narrates in his
autobiography that he heard Dodd preaching on the text:
"If a man look on a woman to lust after her . . ." The text
itself, Carlyle says, was shocking, and the sermon, composed
with the least possible delicacy, was an insult to sincere peni-
tents, and fuel for the passions of hypocrites. So vexed was
Carlyle that when at the close the ladies whispered their
applause, he protested aloud against an address which he
characterized as *contra bonos mores* and a disgrace to Christianity.

After some years of success, money troubles and various
scandals forced Dodd to leave London, and he withdrew to
a living in Buckinghamshire, given him by Lord Chesterfield, the godson and successor to Johnson's patron. Returning to London, Dodd became still further involved in debt,
forged Chesterfield's name to a bond for £4200, and was
arrested.

Dodd had met Johnson only once, twenty-seven years
earlier, when Johnson was coming into fame as the author
of *The Rambler*. Himself handsome and graceful, Dodd was
shocked by Johnson's convulsions and distorted eyes, as he
called them, by his rough, loud voice and obstinate, ungenteel,
and boorish manner. But Johnson's talk impressed him so
much that he could not get him out of his thoughts for some
time after their meeting.

Dodd's appeal to Johnson to intervene on his behalf was
conveyed through Lady Harrington, who sent a letter to
Johnson by Mr. Allen, Johnson's landlord in Bolt Court, and

friend both of Dodd and Johnson. Johnson was much moved by Lady Harrington's letter, and promised to do all he could.

Dr. Dodd's speech at the Old Bailey, before sentence of death was pronounced, his petition to the King, his wife's petition to the Queen, his sermon to his fellow-prisoners, and various other pieces were composed by Johnson, who persevered in his efforts till within two days of the execution, when he urged Lady Harrington to make a last attempt to secure a royal pardon.

The horror with which the English regard any financial dishonesty unprotected by the law was not shared by Johnson, who may also have been influenced by the fact that the man whose purse Dodd tried to lighten was a Chesterfield. In his letter to Dodd on the day before the execution, he wrote: "Be comforted: your crime, morally or religiously considered, has no very deep dye of turpitude. It corrupted no man's principles; it attacked no man's life. It involved only a temporary and reparable injury." To his feeling that the punishment was far too severe for the crime was added his concern for the harm the Church of England would suffer from the execution of one of its ministers. In a letter to one of the Secretaries of State, he wrote: "He is, so far as I can recollect, the first clergyman of our Church who has suffered publick execution for immorality; and I know not whether it would not be more for the interest of religion to bury such an offender in the obscurity of perpetual exile, than to expose him in a cart, and on the gallows, to all who are for any reason enemies to the clergy."

For Dodd himself Johnson had no liking, and though Dodd asked for an interview, Johnson would not go to him. It would, he told Boswell, have done more harm to him than good to Dodd. He was afraid of having his feelings harrowed, and would not expose himself to the ordeal for the sake of a clergyman who had disgraced his cloth, and whom he regarded as a hypocrite. Doubtless his severe repressed nature was repelled by Dodd's effusiveness. "Accept, thou *great* and *good* heart," Dodd wrote to him two days before his execution, "my earnest and fervent thanks and prayers for all thy benevolent and kind efforts in my behalf. Oh, Dr. Johnson! as I sought your knowledge at an early hour in life, would to heaven I had cultivated the love and acquaintance of so excellent a man!" The letter concluded with the hope that when Johnson reached the realms of bliss, Dodd might be there to hail with transports the arrival of his Comforter, his Advocate, and his *Friend*. Although Johnson in his fine and simple reply asked Dodd to offer up a petition for his eternal welfare—a request which, addressed by the great moralist of the age to a convicted forger, shocked many persons—there is a touch of dryness in "those well-intended offices which you are pleased so emphatically to acknowledge." He perhaps did less than justice to the element of sincerity in Dodd, of whom John Wesley said that he had never before seen such a condemned malefactor, and that no one could converse with him without acknowledging that God was with him.

Dodd continued to expect a reprieve up to the last day, but Johnson, in spite of his appeal to Lady Harrington, gave up hope ten days before the execution, and wrote a letter to Allen, which he wished Dodd to read. This letter, which has recently been published for the first time by Dr. R. W. Chapman, illustrates more than any other single document we possess Johnson's two chief characteristics: his sense of the need of the individual to purify himelf against the hour of death, and his interest in human character.

"SIR,—You know that my attention to Dr. Dodd has incited me to inquire what is the real purpose of Government; the dreadful answer I have put in your hands.

"Nothing now remains but that he whose profession it has been to teach others to dye, learns now to dye himself.

"It will be wise to deny admission for this time to all who do not come to assist his preparation; to addict himself wholly to prayer and meditation, and consider himself as no longer connected with the world. He has now nothing to do for the short time that remains, but to reconcile himself to God. To this end it will be proper to abstain totally from all strong liquors, and from all other sensual indulgencies, that his thoughts may be as clear and calm as his condition can allow.

"If his remissions of anguish, and intervals of devotion leave him any time, he may perhaps spend it profitably in writing the history of his own depravation, and marking the gradual declination from innocence and quiet, to that state in which the law has found him. . . . The history of his own mind, if not written by himself, cannot be written, and the instruction that might be derived from it must be lost. . . .

"Let him, however, shut his doors against all hope, all trifles, and all sensuality. . . ."

Apart from its other interest, this letter has an important bearing on Boswell's argument that Johnson's relations with women were at one time not as strict as his principles required. At the close of the Life, Boswell devotes some pages to suggesting that Johnson in his early years in London was, through his association with Savage and others, sometimes hurried into indulgences which he thought criminal. These, Boswell continues, were the sins which caused his frequent expressions of remorse, not such venial trifles as pouring

milk into his tea on Good Friday. Boswell's argument is enveloped in such exalted verbiage that most of his readers
have overlooked the absence of any evidence in support of
it. The two props of his argument are the theory, already
dealt with, that Savage and Johnson pursued prostitutes together, and the fact that Johnson sometimes took a prostitute
to a tavern for a meal. "He owned to many of his friends,"
Boswell writes, "that he used to take women of the town to
taverns, and hear them relate their history. In short, it must
not be concealed that, like many other good and pious men,
among whom we may place the Apostle Paul upon his own
authority, Johnson was not free from propensities which
were ever 'warring against the law of his mind,'—and that in
his combats with them he was sometimes overcome."

The use of the word "owned" is a good example of Boswell's disingenuousness. Johnson, like Gladstone, used to
talk with prostitutes from motives which were consciously
moral, whatever unconscious satisfaction his repressed desires may have received from their confidences. He made no
secret of these talks, was extremely indignant with someone
who misinterpreted their object, and would certainly have
added a stupendous specimen to his anti-Scottish witticisms
had Boswell maintained in his presence that no one would
give a prostitute a meal unless he intended to sleep with her
afterwards.

It is clear from Johnson's Journal, and his exhortations
to Dodd to abstain from sensual indulgences in the solitude
of the condemned cell make it still clearer, that he regarded
any indulgence of sensuality as a sin, and did not consider
avoidance of sexual intercourse as synonymous with chastity.
That his sensual fancies filled him with remorse we know

from several entries in his Journal, and can also infer from the tremendous punishment he inflicted on Boswell when Boswell laughed at his musings on his seraglio. His remorse was strong in proportion to his desire for perfection, and his sufferings over such trivial matters as picturing himself the master of a harem, or putting milk in his tea on Good Friday, sprang not from a false idea of their gravity, but from disgust at his inability to resist temptations which his mind condemned as trivial. That he may also have had a few lapses with women on his conscience is possible, but not likely. He could be abstemious, as he himself said, he could not be temperate; and if he had once broken his resolution against sexual intercourse, he would probably have broken it so often that Boswell would have been able to unearth some real evidence in support of his theory that Johnson, like many other good and pious men, including St. Paul and Boswell, was sometimes overcome in his conflicts with certain propensities.

How severe was Johnson's contest with his sensuality can be seen in a story Mrs. Thrale tells. "One day when my son was going to school, and dear Dr. Johnson followed as far as the garden gate, praying for his salvation, in a voice which those who listened attentively could hear plain enough, he said to me suddenly, 'Make your boy tell you his dreams: the first corruption that entered my heart was communicated in a dream.' 'What was it, Sir?' said I. 'Do not ask me,' he replied, with much violence, and walked away in apparent agitation."

(2)

Such happiness as Johnson derived in his later years from
travel and leisure for talk was balanced by an intensified
sense of the emptiness of existence. Unable to use his vast
powers except under the pressure of want or some extraordinary incentive, he found that he had exchanged the pain
of poverty for the still greater pain of boredom. "It is better,"
he wrote shortly before his death, "that life should struggle
with obstructions, than stagnate and putrefy." The vacuity
of life, Mrs. Thrale says, was his favourite theme, and while
other philosophers found different causes for different
events, Johnson attributed all the exertions of mankind to
the need to pass away the time. "Life must be filled up," he
said to her once, "and the man who is not capable of intellectual pleasures must content himself with such as his senses
afford."

It was only in the heat of talk that his boredom was completely dissipated. The excitement of setting out on a journey
would scatter it for the moment, strange places would stir
his interest for a short time, but on his travels, as at home,
he was not fully alive except in encounters with his fellow-
creatures. The enjoyment he found on his Scottish tour is
in Boswell, who narrates his talk with his various hosts, and
shows him drinking tea with a Highland woman on his knees.
The boredom he suffered is in his *Journey to the Western
Highlands*. He had no sense of beauty in nature or in art,
and looked at the Highlands with a lack-lustre eye. The hills,
he says, by hindering the eye from ranging, forced his mind
to find entertainment for itself. Once only did they move
any interest in him, when his guide told him that what he

took to be a white rock was really snow. "It had already lasted to the end of August," he records, "and was likely to maintain its contest with the sun till it should be reinforced by winter."

The liveliest touch in his narrative sprang from his indignation at the ruined churches in the Hebrides. The Calvinists, he says, attack the lazy devotion of the Romish clergy, but he prefers the sleepy laziness of men who erect churches to the fervid activity of those who suffer them to fall.

He had Boswell to stimulate him on the Scottish tour. The pall of tedium hangs more heavily over his journeys to North Wales and to Paris with the Thrales. When Boswell asked him how his Welsh journey had compared with his Scottish, he replied that he had found green and fertile mountains instead of bleak and barren ones, and that one of the castles of Wales would contain all the castles he had seen in Scotland. This prudent answer put it out of Boswell's power to vex Mrs. Thrale when next they met, but one feels that the baffled Boswell was right when he conjectured that the tour to Wales, though it no doubt contributed to Johnson's health and amusement, did not give an occasion to such a discursive exercise of his mind as the tour to the Hebrides. There is a sentence in Mrs. Thrale's journal of the Welsh tour which brings the heavy plunging old man vividly before our eyes in his vain search for distraction. "We walked up a steep hill they called Wenlock Edge till our feet were very wet and dirty."

Mrs. Thrale's *Journal of the French Tour* in 1775 was published for the first time in 1932 by Mr. Tyson and Mr. Guppy. Johnson, Mrs. Thrale says, loved the very act of travelling, but that in her opinion he loved very little else about travelling appears from her complaint that he took no pleasure in music, painting, or nature. His own notes on the tour show that, though he did not share Mrs. Thrale's enthusiasm for concerts, picture galleries, and scenery, he observed the manners of the French with some attention if little pleasure. Fontainebleau is "a large mean town crowded with people": "Nobody but mean people walk in Paris": "To Versailles—a mean town": "At night we went to a comedy. I neither saw nor heard—drunken women." Only in the menagerie at Versailles does he seem to have been happy, noting in some detail the peculiarities of the various animals, especially of the rhinoceros, a confirmation of Samuel Butler's view that nothing is so soothing to the nerves as to contemplate the larger mammals.

The silences of Johnson, a trait in his character obscured by Boswell, are the chief impression of him left by Mrs. Thrale's account of the journey. One of his friends said of him that he was like a ghost; he never spoke till he was spoken to. Baretti, who went to France with the Thrales, mentions this characteristic with his usual irritable exaggeration: "Johnson was not fit to travel, as every place was equal to him. He mused as much on the road to Paris as he did in his garret in London, as much at a French opera as in his room at Streatham. . . . With men, women, and children he never cared to exchange a word, and if he ever took any delight in anything, it was to converse with some old acquaintance. New people he never loved to be in company with, except ladies when disposed to caress and flatter him."

Johnson's silence during the tour must be read between the lines of Mrs. Thrale's account, though once it obtruded itself so forcibly as to require special comment. The carriage containing Thrale, Baretti, and Hester ran away down a steep hill. Thrale jumped out in order, he later explained, to stop the horses, and nearly broke his leg. The other two did not move, and the horses came to a standstill before over-turning the carriage. "Dr. Johnson's perfect unconcern," Mrs. Thrale wrote on the same day, "for the Lives of three People, who would all have felt for his, shock'd and amaz'd me,—but that, as Baretti says, is true Philosophy; Mrs. Strick-land did not give it so kind a name, I soon saw her indigna-tion towards him prevailing over her Friendship for me." The next day, Mrs. Thrale's agitation having abated, and Johnson having become proportionately more amiable, she wrote: "We have made it all up with Mr. Johnson, who pro-tests it was not unconcern for Mr. Thrale but anger at me that made him sullenly forbear Enquiry when he found me unwilling (as he thought) to give him a ready or rational answer."

His milder mood, when he would amuse himself with any distraction, is shown in another of her entries. "Mr. Johnson has made a little Distich at every Place we have slept at, for example:

A Calais.   St. Omer.   Arras. A Amiens.   Au Mouton.
Trop de frais. Tout est cher. Hélas. On n'a rien. Rien de bon."

(3)

The fundamental cause of his ennui was his inability to harness his energy to steady employment. In the fifteen years after he received his pension, he wrote only one book, *A Journey to the Western Highlands,* and four short political pamphlets, and brought out a revised edition of the Dictionary. Had his faculties decayed after fifty, he would have been less plagued with boredom, but his intellect was as active at seventy as twenty years earlier. The paradox of his life was the combination of vast mental and physical strength with constant sickness of mind and body.

The troubles of his mind do not seem to have grown more severe with age, and fill less space in his Journal during his later years than his physical infirmities. In his sixty-third year he made this entry, which is typical of many entries from this time onwards:

"Of the Spring and Summer (1772), I remember that I was able in those seasons to examine and improve my dictionary, and was seldom withheld from the work but by my own unwillingness. Of my nights I have no distinct remembrance but believe that as in many foregoing years they were painful and restless.

"A little before Christmas I had caught cold, of which at first, as is my custom, I took little notice, but which harassed me as it grew more violent, with a cough almost incessant, both night and day. I was let blood three times, and after about ten weeks, with the help of warm weather, I recovered. From this time I have been much less troubled with nocturnal flatulencies, and have had some nights of that quiet and continual sleep, which I had wanted till I had almost forgotten it.

"O God, grant that I may not misspend or lose the time which thou shalt yet allow me. For Jesus Christ's sake have mercy upon me."

Hardly more than a week of his time was spent altogether on his four political pamphlets. It appears that they were written at the request of the Government, for Johnson complained to a friend that though his pension had been given to him as a literary character, the administration had applied to him to write political pamphlets. As the first of these pamphlets was written more than seven years after the bestowal of the pension, and the other three were spread over the next five years, his grievance lacked weight. It illustrates, however, his attitude to authority. He despised democracy and believed in authority, but his idea of authority was a power which regulated the machinery of life without interfering much with the ordinary individual or at all with Samuel Johnson. "I would not," he once said, "give half a guinea to live under one form of government rather than another. It is of no moment to the happiness of an individual. Sir, the abuse of power is nothing to a private man. . . . If a sovereign oppresses his people to a great degree, they will rise and cut off his head. There is a remedy in human nature against tyranny that will keep us safe under every form of government." These are the cheerful views of a man who lived during the reigns of monarchs with a precarious title to their thrones. England in Johnson's time was factious and high-spirited. Johnson regretted this factiousness and approved Chatham as a dictator who possessed the power of putting the State in motion. Had he lived under a real dictator, like Cromwell, he would have been less enthusiastic about arbitrary power.

More to the point are his remarks on the opposite evil of mob government. When Boswell questioned the advantage of returning to the old system, under which the City appointed its Mayors by seniority, Johnson replied: "The evil of competition is greater than that of the worst Mayor that can come; besides, there is no more reason to suppose that the choice of a rabble will be right, than that chance will be right." His account of a popular petition in *The*

False Alarm, his anti-Wilkes pamphlet, is as amusing as Swift. "The progress of a petition is well known. . . . Meat and drink are plentifully provided; a crowd is easily brought together. . . . The petition is read and universally approved. Those who are sober enough to write, add their names, and the rest would sign it if they could. . . . The poor loiterer, whose shop had confined him, or whose wife had locked him up, hears the tale of luxury with envy, and at last inquires what was their petition. Of the petition nothing is remembered by the narrator, but that it spoke much of fears and apprehensions, and something very alarming, and that he is sure it is against the Government; the other is convinced that it must be right, and wishes he had been there, for he loves wine and venison, and is resolved as long as he lives to be against the Government."

What Johnson himself would have been like, had he risen to supreme power, and lost his wisdom and humanity on the way, is shown in his attack on the American colonists in *Taxation No Tyranny.* A single sentence will be enough to depict him in his Cromwell-sacking-Drogheda mood: "When he (the Englishman) is told through what extent of territory he must traverse to subdue them, he recollects how far, a few years ago, he travelled in their defence. When it is urged that they will shoot up like the hydra, he naturally considers how the hydra was destroyed."

In 1777 Johnson was drawn into an undertaking which, modest in its first design, gradually enlarged itself, becoming at last his longest and in some respects most important contribution to English literature. Approached by a group of booksellers to write a series of short notices for a standard collection of the English poets, he accepted the commission, and completed it in three years, writing, he says, in his usual way, dilatorily and hastily, unwilling to work, and working with vigour and haste. With a lifetime of reading and knowledge of literary history to draw on, Johnson soon overflowed the limits suggested by the booksellers, and while dealing perfunctorily with many of the lesser writers, produced about half a dozen studies which have not been surpassed in our literature for acuteness of social and moral criticism.

Like *The Rambler,* the *Lives of the Poets* were written to promote piety, and, like *The Rambler,* are most instructive when least instructing. That his piety warped his sense of literature seems occasionally to have suggested itself to Johnson, for he opens his sketch of Dr. Watts with: "The poems of Dr. Watts were by my recommendation inserted in the late collection; the readers of which are to impute to me whatever pleasure or weariness they may find in the perusal of Blackmore, Watts, Pomfret, and Yalden."

The æsthetic criticism in the *Lives* shows Johnson's usual limitations. Though he could feel, he could not interpret the greatness of Shakespeare and Milton, and he could not even feel the more recondite beauty of Donne. Yet though he has little of value to say about the highest forms of poetry, he clears away all imitations of sublimity with a vigorous hand. "Where truth is sufficient to fill the mind," he says of Gray's Odes, "fiction is worse than useless; the counterfeit debases the genuine. . . . To select a singular event, and swell it to a giant's bulk by fabulous appendages of spectres and predictions, has little difficulty; for he that forsakes the probable may always find the marvellous."

This attack on Gray, and his strictures on Milton and

others, were violently resented in some quarters. Cowper, on reading Johnson's Milton, exclaimed: "Oh! I could thresh his old jacket till I made his pension jingle in his pocket"; and Anna Seward cried out against the "turbulent fierceness and jealousy of his unbridled passions," and repeatedly urged that envy was the sole cause of his harshness to Milton, Gray, Collins, Prior, and others of her favourites.

Johnson was irked by the stout and effusive Anna, told her once that he would hang a dog that read "Lycidas" twice, and when she said, "What, then, must become of me, who can say it by heart?" retorted, "Die in a surfeit of bad taste." Her attacks on him must therefore be discounted, but she had far more taste and sensitiveness to good poetry than has generally been allowed, and was understandably chilled by the severe tone which pervades the *Lives*. Where she was mistaken was in supposing, like most readers, that severity in writing implies an absence of generous feeling. The writers who are most generous on paper are usually the most prudent in life, and the reverse is equally true. On examining the *Lives*, one finds that, concise though Johnson is in praise, he has never withheld it where he felt it to be due, except perhaps with Swift, for whom he had an aversion founded on doubt of his sincerity as a Christian, disgust at his obscenity, and contempt for his railings at a world which had given him a fair measure of applause. The glow of youthful enthusiasm is not to be expected in a man of seventy. It is rather to be wondered at that Johnson had preserved so profound a love for literature through the oppression of his life. To his masters, Dryden, Pope, and Addison, he gives more than their due, and though he detested Milton's politics, he praises him as a poet in one of his noblest sentences:

"His great works were performed under discountenance, and in blindness, but difficulties vanished at his touch; he was born for whatever is arduous; and his work is not the greatest of heroic poems, only because it is not the first."

The sardonic wisdom of the *Lives,* which a few examples will illustrate, gives them their chief interest and permanent value.

"The man who threatens the world is always ridiculous; for the world can easily go on without him, and in a short time will cease to miss him. I have heard of an idiot who used to revenge his vexations by lying all night upon the bridge."

"He that asks a subscription soon finds that he has enemies. All who do not encourage him defame him. He that wants money will rather be thought angry than poor; and he that wishes to save his money conceals his avarice by his malice."

"His (Pope's) scorn of the Great is repeated too often to be real; no man thinks much of that which he despises."

"Abraham Cowley was born in the year 1618. His father was a grocer, whose condition Dr. Sprat conceals under the general appellation of a citizen."

Two longer extracts will show, the first that a great tragic writer, the second that another Rabelais, were concealed in Johnson:

THE DEATH OF SWIFT

"He grew more violent; and his mental powers declined, till (1741) it was found necessary that legal guardians should be appointed of his person and fortune. He now lost distinction. His madness was compounded of rage and fatuity. The last face that he knew was that of Mrs. Whiteway; and her he ceased to know in a little time. His meat was brought to him cut into mouthfuls; but he would never touch it while the servant stayed, and at last, after it had stood perhaps an hour, would eat it walking; for he continued his old habit, and was on his feet ten hours a day.

". . . A short interval of reason ensuing, in which he knew his physician and his family, gave hopes of his recovery; but in a few days he sunk into lethargic stupidity, motionless, heedless, and speechless. But it is said, that, after a year of total silence, when his housekeeper, on the thirtieth of November, told him that the usual bonfires and illuminations were preparing to cele- brate his birthday, he answered, 'It is all folly; they had better let it alone.'

"It is remembered, that he afterwards spoke now and then, or gave some intimation of a meaning; but at last sunk into a perfect silence, which continued till about the end of October 1745, when, in his seventy-eighth year, he expired without a struggle."

THE DEATH OF EDMUND SMITH

"Having formed his plan (a tragedy on Lady Jane Grey) and collected materials, he declared that a few months would com- plete his design; and, that he might pursue his work with less frequent avocations, he was, in June 1710, invited by Mr. George Ducket to his house at Hartham, in Wiltshire. Here he found such opportunities of indulgence as did not much forward his studies, and particularly some strong ale, too delicious to be resisted. He ate and drank till he found himself plethoric; and, then resolving to ease himself by evacuation, he wrote to an apothecary in the neighbourhood a prescription of a purge so forcible, that the apothecary thought it his duty to delay it till he had given notice of its danger. Smith, not pleased with the contradiction of a shopman, and boastful of his own knowledge, treated the notice with rude contempt, and swallowed his own medicine, which, in July 1710, brought him to the grave. He was buried at Hartham."

CHAPTER EIGHT

"The Gulphs of Fate"

(1)

IN the summer of 1778 Fanny Burney, who was staying at Streatham, noted in her journal that Mr. Thrale was ill and in poor spirits. "Indeed," she adds, "he seems not to be a happy man, though he has every means of happiness in his power. . . ." Two or three days later she writes of him coming in from an election dinner so tired out that he neither opened his eyes nor mouth, but fell asleep directly after tea.

Thrale, though not yet fifty, was breaking up, but no one saw anything unusual in his lethargy, and Johnson himself was enjoying some of the happiest hours of his life in the society of Fanny Burney, whom his praise of *Evelina,* a few months earlier, had delighted so much that when her friend, old Mr. Crisp, brought her the news of it she danced a jig under a mulberry tree, "without any preparation, music, or explanation."

"I have had a thousand delightful conversations with Dr. Johnson," she records in the September of 1778. ". . . Whenever he is below stairs he keeps me a prisoner, for he does not like I should quit the room for a moment; if I rise, he constantly calls out, 'Don't you go, little Burney!' "

One day Mrs. Thrale announced that Mrs. Montagu was

coming to dinner. "Dr. Johnson," Fanny Burney writes, "began to see-saw with a countenance strongly expressive of in-
ward fun, and after enjoying it for some time in silence, he
suddenly, and with great animation, turned to me and cried,
'Down with her, Burney!—down with her!—spare her not!—
attack her, fight her, and down with her at once! You are a
rising wit, and she is at the top; and when I was beginning
the world, and was nothing and nobody, the joy of my life
was to fire at all the established wits! and then everybody
loved to halloo me on. But there is no game now; everybody
would be glad to see me conquered: but then, when I was
new, to vanquish the great ones was all the delight of my
poor little soul! So at her, Burney—at her, and down with
her!' "

Thrale's health grew worse, and in June 1779 he had a
stroke. In the spring of 1780 Johnson wrote to Mrs. Thrale,
urging that Mr. Thrale should decide on a diet and stick
to it. But no advice could curb what Mrs. Thrale calls his
"preternatural desire for food." Early in 1781 he was warned
that his life was in danger and that he must go into the country. "Leave London! Lose my Ranelagh season!" he cried,
and refused to hear the suggestion again. His vanishing
strength was applied to the organization of a large entertainment. The musical side of the entertainment he placed in
the charge of Piozzi, a distinguished Italian musician, but
the chief attraction was to be a Brahmin and two Parsees.

A few days before his death he begged Sir Philip Jennings
Clerke to write to his brother, the Prebendary of Worcester,
to request for Thrale the first lampreys the Severn should
produce that season; but before the lampreys could arrive

he had a second stroke, and died on the day fixed for the entertainment, April 4, 1781.

That "Nature sets her gifts on the right hand and on the left" was a truth which Johnson had expressed in *Rasselas,* but the application of which to his own position with Mrs. Thrale after her husband's death he did not at once realize. During Thrale's life Johnson had preferred the gift of ease to the gift of independence. When Thrale died he grasped at both gifts, expecting to enjoy the comforts with which Thrale had required Mrs. Thrale to provide him, and the unconstraint of a house no longer dominated by Thrale.

If Mrs. Thrale had been in love with him, his expectation would have been reasonable, and it is possible that, half-consciously, he had hopes of marrying her. Fanny Burney records that shortly after Thrale's death, Johnson gave more care to his dress, bought silver buckles for his shoes, and grew daily gayer and gayer, and more cheerful and pleasant. But when Thrale's brewery had been sold, Johnson began to see his mistake. It was the sale of the brewery which made Mrs. Thrale conscious of her freedom. By it, she wrote in her journal, she had purchased peace and a stable fortune, restoration to her original rank in life, and a situation undisturbed by commercial jargon, unpolluted by commercial frauds, and undisgraced by commercial connexions. She was free, she was wealthy, and forty was not too late an age for happiness.

Johnson had no place in the pictures of happiness which her growing love of Piozzi was beginning to evoke. Though she had affection and a deep respect for him, he was too closely connected with the dreariness of her life with Thrale,

whose authority he had always supported. Above all, association with him made her more conscious of her age and
of the inappropriateness in a woman who had borne twelve
children of expecting romance and passion from the future.
Johnson, in short, symbolized for her everything from which
she wished to escape, while she stood to Johnson for everything which during many years had made life endurable, and
might now make it more than merely endurable.

Accustomed so long to submit her will to another's, and
having little natural dignity or self-possession, Mrs. Thrale
was neither firm nor gracious with Johnson in this difficult
situation. She had not the heart nor as yet the wish to sever
their connexion, and equally she lacked the tact and self-
confidence to transform their relations into those of ordinary
friendship.

The position was made more embarrassing by the newspapers, which shortly after Thrale's death began to speculate
about whom his widow would marry, naming among other
possible candidates Sir Richard Jebb, George Selwyn, Johnson, and Piozzi. How she dealt with this embarrassment, she
records in her journal with some consciousness that she had
not improved a delicate situation. "Somebody mentioned my
going to be married t'other day, and Johnson was joking
about it. 'I suppose, Sir,' said I, 'they think they are doing
me honour with their imaginary matches when, perhaps, the
man does not exist who would do me honour by marrying
me!' This, indeed, was said in the wild and insolent spirit
of Baretti, yet, 'tis nearer the truth than one would think
for. A woman of passable person, ancient family, respectable
character, uncommon talents, and three thousand a year,
has a right to think herself any man's equal, and has nothing

to seek but return of affection from whatever partner she pitches on. To marry for love would therefore be rational in me, who want no other advancement in birth or fortune, and *till I am in love,* I will not marry, nor perhaps then."

Johnson now began to regret Thrale, for whom, however mixed its nature, his affection had been great. Writing to a friend, nearly a year after Thrale's death, he said that his life had been mournful of late. In the spring of the previous year he had lost Thrale, and for such another friend the general course of human things would not suffer a man to hope. He had passed the summer at Streatham, but there was no Thrale; and having idled away the summer with a weakly body and neglected mind had journeyed to Staffordshire on the edge of winter, sickly himself and finding the friends sickly whom he went to see.

Mrs. Thrale meanwhile was falling more and more in love with Piozzi, whom she had first met at a party at Dr. Burney's. That she was at once affected by him appears from Fanny Burney's account of her curious but not inexplicable behaviour, when he sat down to the piano. He had his back to the company, and Mrs. Thrale, stealing up behind him on tiptoe, began to imitate his playing, squaring her elbows, elevating them with ecstatic shrugs of her shoulders, and casting up her eyes, while languishingly inclining her head.

A little later, seven months before Thrale's death, they met at Brighton. Mrs. Thrale's interest in Piozzi had been encouraged by Fanny Burney, who praised Piozzi as a man just to Mrs. Thrale's taste, a companion who would lighten the burden of life to her. Encountering him in a library at Brighton, Mrs. Thrale asked him to give Hester singing lessons, and within a few days was writing in her journal:

"Piozzi is become a prodigious favourite with me, he is so intelligent a creature, so discerning, one can't help wishing for his good opinion . . . his hand on the pianoforte, too, is so soft, so sweet, so delicate, every tone goes to the heart, I think, and fills the mind with emotions one would not be without, though inconvenient sometimes."

Half in love with him before Thrale died, her passion grew quickly during the summer which Johnson passed so unhappily at Streatham, and was intensified by the fear of losing him when he was summoned to Paris to play before Marie Antoinette. "I have got my Piozzi home at last," she wrote in November; "he looks thin and battered, but always kindly upon me, I think."

While she was waiting for Piozzi to return, Johnson was wandering drearily through the Midlands. "All here is gloomy," he wrote to her from Lichfield in October; "a faint struggle with the tediousness of time; a doleful confession of present misery, and the approach seen and felt of what is most dreaded and shunned." From Lichfield he went to Taylor, at Ashbourne, where he heard from Mrs. Thrale that Piozzi was returning to Streatham. "When *he* comes and *I* come," he replied, "you will have two about you that will love you; and I question if either of us heartily care how few more you have." He still looked on Streatham as his home, and his letters on his way back, through Birmingham, Lichfield, and London, almost openly entreat Mrs. Thrale to welcome him as in old days. "You have got Piozzi back," he wrote in one. ". . . Pray contrive a multitude of things for us to do when we meet. Something that may *hold all together;* though if anything makes *me* love you more, it is going from you"; and in another letter: "Do not neglect me, nor relinquish me. Nobody will ever love you better or honour you more. . . ."

When he reached Streatham, Mrs. Thrale noted the arrival of "dear Mr. Johnson," and expressed a fear that he might become paralytic, some symptoms being already discernible about his mouth; but her growing impatience with him is made clear. Queeney is working hard with him at the classics, she says, and adds: "I hope she will be *out* of leading strings at least before *he* gets into them."

As he felt the breach between himself and Mrs. Thrale widening, his thoughts turned to his other friends, and at the beginning of the new year, 1782, he wrote with unusual tenderness to Boswell: "I sit down to answer your letter on the same day in which I received it, and am pleased that my first letter of the year is to you. . . . Shall we ever have another frolick like our journey to the Hebrides? I hope that dear Mrs. Boswell will surmount her complaints; in losing her you would lose your anchor, and be tost, without stability, by the waves of life. I wish both her and you very many years, and very happy." Some days later, sitting in his bedroom at Streatham, he thought of Levett, and resolved with uncommon earnestness, as he afterwards wrote to Langton, that whatever changes came into his life, and wherever he might go, he would try to keep Levett with him. In the morning Francis Barber brought him the news that Levett had died during the night.

The deep emotion and the absolute sincerity with which Johnson had written of Peyton's death appear again in his verses on the death of Levett.

> "Condemn'd to Hope's delusive mine,
> As on we toil from day to day,

By sudden blast or slow decline
  Our social comforts drop away.

Well tried through many a varying year,
  See Levett to the grave descend;
Officious, innocent, sincere,
  Of every friendless name the friend.

Yet still he fills affection's eye,
  Obscurely wise, and coarsely kind,
Nor, letter'd arrogance, deny
  Thy praise to merit unrefin'd.

When fainting Nature call'd for aid,
  And hov'ring Death prepar'd the blow,
His vigorous remedy display'd
  The power of art without the show.

In Misery's darkest caverns known,
  His ready help was ever nigh,
Where hopeless Anguish pour'd his groan,
  And lonely Want retir'd to die.

No summons mock'd by chill delay,
  No petty gains disdain'd by pride;
The modest wants of every day,
  The toil of every day supplied.

His virtues walked their narrow round,
  Nor made a pause, nor left a void;
And sure the Eternal Master found
  His single talent well employ'd.

The busy day, the peaceful night,
  Unfelt, uncounted, glided by;
His frame was firm, his powers were bright,
  Though now his eightieth year was nigh.

> Then, with no throbs of fiery pain,
> No cold gradations of decay,
> Death broke at once the vital chain,
> And freed his soul the nearest way."

The reference to social comforts in the first verse, and to Levett's quick and painless death in the last, reflect the two fears which were now oppressing Johnson. Returning very ill to London, he wrote to Mrs. Thrale at the end of January that he had been bled and hoped soon to be well enough to visit her, but if he came now he would only cough and cough. "We are here all three sick, and poor Levett is gone. Do not add to my other distress any diminution of kindness. . . ."

Meanwhile Mrs. Thrale's position was increasingly difficult. She knew that everyone would cry out against a marriage with Piozzi, an Italian, a musician, and a Catholic; and being herself dominated by conventional prejudices, she lacked for the time being the courage to ignore public opinion. Nor was she yet equal to defying Johnson. Her distracted state appears in her note on Johnson's return to Streatham in February: "Here is Mr. Johnson ill, very ill indeed, and—I do not see what ails him; 'tis repelled gout, I fear, fallen on the lungs and breath of course. What shall we do for him? If I lose him, I am more than undone: friend, father, guardian, confidant!—God give me health and patience. What shall I do?"

During the next few months Johnson, when he was away from Streatham, wrote as usual to Mrs. Thrale, but not with his old easiness. His tone, whether he is affectionate or vivacious, is generally forced. One letter begins: "Dearest of all dear Ladies"; another, "Yesterday I was all so bonny, as who but me?"; a third, "Wisely was it said by him who said it

first, that this world is all ups and downs." But sometimes
his real feeling is shown, and once he begs her not to let Mr.
Piozzi or anybody else put him quite out of her mind, or
think that anybody will love her as he does.

His health was now so bad that Mrs. Thrale expected his
death to solve the problem of his inevitable opposition to
her marriage with Piozzi. The opposition of the rest of her
circle she hoped to circumvent by going to Italy with Piozzi
and her daughters, winning her daughters to her side while
in Italy and confronting society with an accomplished fact
on her return. How far her plans were discussed with Piozzi
is not known, nor even if their love for one another had been
declared at this date, the summer of 1782. That Piozzi was
punctilious in money matters, prudent, sensitive, honourable, and, in short, everything that an Italian musician woo-
ing a rich English widow might reasonably have been expected not to be, we know. We know, too, that he made her
an excellent husband, and thereby disappointed the forebod-
ings of all her friends. But whether he directed events, or
merely submitted to them, rode the storm or was blown before it, is impossible to say. Cecilia, Mrs. Thrale's youngest
daughter, writing to her mother some years after her marriage with Piozzi, quotes what was perhaps his most frequent
expression about the countrymen of his wife: "My godda
bless, never I see such a people." He had full reason to use
it during his lifetime, and if he returned to this world would
certainly use it again on learning that his wife was still being
abused for entering on a second marriage which proved as
happy as her first was miserable.

As Johnson did not die, Mrs. Thrale, who knew that Johnson longed to see Italy, was at a loss what to do. To travel

with him, she says, *she* could not bear, and to leave him behind *he* could not bear. But when at last she mentioned the Italian project to him, he approved of it cordially, expressed no wish to go with her, and said he hoped he would live to see her return in two or three years. Her vanity was hurt by his calmness, though she exaggerated her annoyance in order to whip up her courage against him. "He feels nothing in parting with me," she wrote, "nothing in the least; but thinks it a prudent scheme, and goes to his books as usual. . . . I begin to see that Johnson's connexion with me is merely an interested one. . . . Yet I really thought he could not have existed without my conversation *forsooth!* He cares more for my roast beef and plum pudden, which he now devours too dirtily for endurance; and since he is glad to get rid of me, I'm sure I have good cause to desire the getting rid of him."

The Italian journey fell through, and as the next best step to cutting free from her old life Mrs. Thrale decided to leave Streatham, which in October 1782 she let to Lord Shelburne. She had been during some months irritable and ill-at-ease with her old friends. "Sad and altered Streatham," Dr. Burney called it, and left it one day in tears, one's sympathy for his distress being, however, lessened by his horror at the widow of a brewer falling in love with a distinguished member of his own profession. Another day, Johnson and Fanny Burney travelled up to town together, and as they drove away from Streatham, Johnson pointed at the house with a shaking hand and exclaimed, "That house is lost to *me* for ever!"

On October 7, he records in his Journal, he packed up his bundles, read for the last time in the library at Streatham, and after breakfast prayed with Mrs. Thrale and the children, commending them to the protection of God, and asking for grace to remember with thankfulness the comforts and conveniences he had enjoyed at Streatham, and to resign them with submission.

There was no open breach between him and Mrs. Thrale, and he joined her towards the end of October at Brighton, in such a state of weakness that he had to rest four times between the coaching inn and his lodgings. As his strength came back, rage succeeded to resignation, and during his stay at Brighton he was so savage to everyone, friends and strangers alike, that he was excluded from the invitations sent to Mrs. Thrale.

Meanwhile the secret tension between Hester Thrale and her mother had snapped, and the battle over Piozzi had opened. "I am not to think about myself," Mrs. Thrale wrote: "I married the first time to please my mother, I must marry the second time to please my daughter; let me rise to the rank of a human being conscious of its own power to discern good from ill. The person who has uniformly acted by the will of others has hardly that dignity to boast."

Thrale had left his five daughters £20,000 each. They had guardians to look after their interests, and Hester, who was now eighteen, was cool, resolute, and experienced in worldly matters. Since Thrale's death, she had assumed the headship of the family, her sisters looking to her for guidance, not to their mother, whose subjection to their father had deprived her of authority over them. The picture, drawn by a long succession of writers, of Mrs. Thrale abandoning her fatherless and unprotected children to the chances and perils of life, is the exact reverse of the truth. It was her daughters, led by Hester, who forced on her the alternatives of exile with Piozzi or England without him, and who, when she chose the former, attracted to themselves the sympathy and concern of society as a whole.

Hester no doubt thought the ardours of her mother ridiculous and undignified; but her chief objection to the marriage was that it might compromise her own social position, and so lessen her chances of a good match. That Mrs. Thrale invited, and in some degree justified, her daughter's contempt by trying to conciliate her, is undeniable. If Mrs. Thrale had had more character, and been herself less troubled about the opinion of society, she would have married Piozzi without consulting anyone.

The battle between Hester and her mother raged from October 1782 till April 1783; and though the next two sisters, Susan and Sophy, did not join in actively, they taught the two youngest girls to cry, "Where are you going, mama? Will you leave us and die as our poor papa did?" and whenever Piozzi called, all the girls would run away, Mrs. Thrale laments, as if they saw a serpent.

Towards the close of January, Fanny Burney called on Mrs. Thrale and told her in front of Hester that if she wished to keep her reputation, she must either marry Piozzi at once or give him up. Mrs. Thrale threw herself groaning on her bed, perhaps hoping to move Hester, who looked on impassively. "She had indeed never," Mrs. Thrale says, "by one tender word endeavoured to dissuade me from the match, but said coldly that if I *would* abandon the children, I *must;* that their father had not deserved such treatment from me; that I should be punished by Piozzi's neglect, for that she knew he hated me; and that I turned out my offspring to chance for his sake, like puppies in a pond to swim or drown as Providence pleased; that for her part she must look herself out a place like the other servants, for my face would she never see more. 'Nor write to me?' said I. 'I shall not, Madam,' replied she with a cold sneer, 'easily find out your address; for you are going you know not whither, I believe.' "

A few weeks later Mrs. Thrale and Piozzi became engaged, an act of desperation on her part, which redoubled her daughter's attacks. In April she gave way. It was agreed between her and Piozzi that he should return to Italy, and they met for the last time in London, in the house in Argyll Street to which she had now moved. "God give me strength to part with him courageously," she wrote on April 6; "I expect him every instant to breakfast with me for the *last* time. Gracious Heavens, what words are these! Oh no, for mercy may we meet again! without diminished kindness. Oh, my love, my love!"

Piozzi begged to see her once more, but she could not face another interview. "I never knew," she wrote later, "till Piozzi told me after he returned to England, that he had been sitting at a front window of some public-house on the road all that dreadful Sunday, to see my carriage pass backwards and forwards to where the children resided. Oh, what moments! Oh, what moments!"

Two or three weeks before the parting of Mrs. Thrale and Piozzi, Boswell called on Johnson, who was staying with Mrs. Thrale in Argyll Street, and found Mrs. Thrale apparently as attentive to him as formerly. His health was now very bad; he looked pale, Boswell says, and had a difficulty with his breathing. The strength and combativeness which had sustained him through his life were ebbing. "I wonder," he said to Boswell, after a long silence, "how I should have any enemies; for I do harm to nobody." A few weeks later Hannah More noticed the change in him: "Poor Johnson exerted himself exceedingly; but he was very ill and looked so dreadfully, that it quite grieved me. His sickness seems to have softened his mind, without having at all weakened it."

In the middle of June he had a paralytic stroke, waking up in the night to find his power of speech gone. Two days later, writing to Mrs. Thrale, who had left London for Bath, he said that his speech had almost returned, and that his memory was unimpaired, but that he was uncertain what other faculties might not be attacked. "How this will be received by you," he wrote, "I know not. I hope you will sympathize with me. . . . I have loved you with virtuous affection; I have honoured you with sincere esteem. Let not all our endearments be forgotten, but let me have in this great distress your pity and your prayers. You see I yet turn to you with my complaints as a settled and inalienable friend; do not, do not drive me from you, for I have not deserved either neglect or hatred. . . . O God! give me comfort and confidence in Thee: forgive my sins; and if it be Thy good pleasure, relieve my diseases for Jesus Christ's sake. Amen."

He was consoled by Mrs. Thrale's reply, and wrote to her again.

Mrs. Desmoulins and her daughter were no longer with him, Polly Carmichael had long since vanished, Levett was dead; and Miss Williams, he now told Mrs. Thrale, was so weak that she could no longer be a companion to him. "When I rise, my breakfast is solitary, the black dog waits to share it, from breakfast to dinner he continues barking, except that Dr. Brocklesby for a little keeps him at a distance. Dinner with a sick woman you may venture to suppose not much better than solitary. After dinner, what remains but to count the clock, and hope for that sleep which I can scarce expect. Night comes at last, and some hours of restlessness and confusion bring me again to a day of solitude. Who shall exclude the black dog from a habitation like this?"

Miss Williams's temper grew worse as she approached her end. One day towards the close of August when Johnson went into her room to ask how she was, she answered so savagely that he withdrew very downcast, and wrote to tell Hester of her unkindness. "She saw," he said, "that my tenderness put it in her power to give me pain." Unable to bear her temper, he went to a friend at Heale, near Salisbury. A few days later Miss Williams was dead. In writing to Mrs. Thrale of her death, Johnson quoted two lines from the dirge in *Cymbeline,* putting "weary" for "worldly," perhaps unconsciously:

> "Thou thy weary task hast done,
>   Home art gone, and ta'en thy wages."

In his letter to Hester, Johnson said that he had seldom had so little to do with Boswell as of late. Since Boswell's visit to London in the spring, he said, Boswell had written to him only twice. He added that he had written to Boswell only once.

That Boswell was cooling off Johnson in Johnson's last years has sometimes been darkly hinted at. More even than most great men, Johnson is considered by posterity to have had the first claim on the attention of all his friends. Boswell was now middle-aged: drink, women, a chaos of uncompleted projects, and a fretful wife had taken much of the glow out of life; his ardour for everything was abated. But that his ardour for Johnson was disproportionately abated there is no convincing evidence. With his awe for Johnson there had always been mixed a discreetly concealed feeling of superiority in certain respects, notably birth, personal charm, and experience of the other sex. As these superiorities seemed to him to have escaped Johnson, his vanity was hurt. The maulings he suffered at Johnson's hands increased his resentment, and this resentment produced the only extant piece of evidence which can be interpreted as a sign that his affection for Johnson was seriously impaired towards the close.

Boswell's "Ode by Dr. Samuel Johnson to Mrs. Thrale upon their supposed approaching nuptials" was written shortly after Thrale's death, and published anonymously in 1788 with a preface. It has not been reprinted, and the only surviving copy is in the Dyce Collection at the South Kensington Museum.

In the preface Boswell describes Johnson as a "very large man, and by no means well-looking, but rather the contrary; neither was he neat and cleanly in his person and dress." He goes on to say that there was no over-delicate niceness between Mrs. Thrale and Johnson, but truly the plainest familiarity, and suggests that Johnson's frequent references to Dr. Taylor's bull had a symbolic significance for Mrs. Thrale, whom he also implies to have been on too familiar terms with Baretti. The Ode itself he attributes to Johnson, and says that he is publishing it for Johnson's sake, to counteract the injurious effect of the ribald verse poured out in the press about Johnson and Mrs. Thrale. "I am well assured by a person of skill," he says, "that they have the

undoubted sterling mark, and that no other man in the kingdom could make them but himself."

All this is on the far side of good taste, and goes some way
to disprove Boswell's contention that "un gentilhomme est
toujours gentilhomme." But to someone so muddled as Boswell it is probable that his Ode and its preface did really
seem to combine the merits of a lively *jeu d'esprit* and a
valuable counterblast to the poetasters of the press, to be at
the same time a reprisal for many insults and a vindication
of Johnson's elevated sentiments for Mr. Thrale's widow. He
did not, it is true, go so far as to show the Ode to Johnson,
and was much alarmed when Wilkes threatened to send
Johnson a copy, but he was proud enough of it to refer to it
in the Life as "a poem not without characteristical merit."

A few verses will show that there is nothing more sinister
in the Ode than a strain of maudlin malice, softened by
maudlin sympathy for the fevers of asceticism, and further
qualified by the attribution to Johnson's passion for Mrs.
Thrale of what in the argument prefixed to the poem Boswell
calls "the delicate sanction of sentiment."

> ". . . To rich felicity thus rais'd,
>   My bosom glows with amorous fire;
> Porter no longer shall be prais'd;
>   'Tis I MYSELF am *Thrale's entire!*
>
>   .   .   .   .   .   .
>
> Ascetick now thy lover lives,
>   Nor dares to touch, nor dares to kiss;
> Yet prurient fancy sometimes gives
>   A prelibation of our bliss.
>
> Convuls'd in love's tumultuous throws,
>   We feel the aphrodisian spasm;

Tir'd nature must, at last, repose,
    Then Wit and Wisdom fill the chasm.

Nor only are our limbs entwin'd,
    And lip in rapture glued to lip;
Lock'd in embraces of the mind;
    Imagination's sweets we sip.

Five daughters by a former spouse
    Shall match with nobles of the land;
The fruit of our more fervent vows
    A pillar of the State shall stand."

(2)

The passing months did not reconcile Mrs. Thrale to the separation from Piozzi, and though she continued to correspond with Johnson she saw in him one of the chief obstacles to her happiness, and found the task of forcing sympathy with his ill-health increasingly irksome. Had he been able to judge the situation with detachment, he would for every reason, selfish and unselfish, have told her to recall Piozzi. But, unreasonable as King Lear, he nursed his growing resentment.

The right of the individual, within the limits imposed by his own conscience, to act without regard to the prejudices and conventions of society was one of Johnson's deepest convictions. "Disdain to regulate your own practice by the practice of another, or by any other principle than the desire of doing right," he wrote to Boswell. He approved Taylor's separation from his wife, he was always opposed to the tyranny of parents over children, and he was equally opposed to the sacrifice of parents to their children. "I entreat you to take care of yourself," he once wrote to Mrs. Thrale.

"Whatever number of boys and girls you may give us, we are far from being certain that any of them will ever do for us what you can do." But now, half in jealousy, half in wounded vanity that Mrs. Thrale should desire to elevate an Italian fiddler to the place once held by his "master," he was ready to join with the rest of the social herd in attacking a mother who by marrying for love might make it harder for her daughters to marry for position.

One day in the autumn of 1783 Fanny Burney called on Johnson, and they talked for a while on general matters. Suddenly he fell silent, his face became stern, and he began to see-saw to and fro, his eyes fixed on the fire. He had never mentioned Piozzi's name to her, but now he could no longer contain himself, and, turning abruptly to her, hoarsely ejaculated—"Piozzi!" "He evidently," she continues, "intended to say more; but the effort with which he articulated that name robbed him of any voice for amplification, and his whole frame grew tremulously convulsed. At length, and with great agitation, he broke forth with: 'She cares for no one. You only—you, she loves still. But no one—and nothing else. You she still loves——' A half-smile now, though of no very gay character, softened a little the severity of his features, while he tried to resume some cheerfulness in adding: 'as—she loves her little finger.' "

Except for his Negro servant, he was now alone in Bolt Court. During the day he had many visitors, and received presents of venison, pheasant, and turkey. But the solitude of his nights oppressed him, and his health was growing worse. "I am in a state, I think, to be pitied, if pity be a passion ever to come into use," he wrote to Hester at the end of September 1783. His gout, he said, had been so painful that he could not without many expedients and repeated efforts raise himself in bed. A brief improvement in his health a few weeks later allowed him to look round for some diversion, and he tried to revive the club which had met at Horseman's, in Ivy Lane, more than thirty years earlier. An old fellow-member, Mr. Ryland, went to Ivy Lane, but Horseman was dead and the inn shut up. Another inn was chosen, and on December 13, the Ivy Lane survivors, Johnson, Hawkins, Ryland, and Payne, met for supper. At ten, Hawkins relates, they broke up, much to the regret of Johnson, who, when he could not persuade them to sit longer, walked away "with a sigh that seemed to come from his heart."

On the following day he was attacked by asthma, which became so severe that he had often to sit all night in his chair, being unable to breathe without great pain when he lay down. Dropsy supervened, and he felt that death was approaching.

One day, when Hawkins called on him, he asked him to draw near, as he wished to enter into a serious conversation. Hawkins was not easily moved, and says elsewhere that he wondered at Johnson choosing him for a confessor, a part for which he was, he admits, meanly qualified. But he was cut to the heart by Johnson's look as he said that he had the prospect of death before him, and dreaded to meet his Saviour. Hawkins tried to reassure him, begging him to reflect on the services he had rendered to the cause of religion and virtue; but Johnson answered that though he had written like a philosopher, he had not lived like one, and broke into a passionate cry, "Shall I, who have been a teacher of others, myself be a castaway?"

Weeks passed without any relief of the asthma, and with an increase of the dropsy. One day in the third week of February 1784, he told Francis to admit no one. "Your master," he said, "is preparing himself to die." When Hawkins called the next morning, he was astonished at Johnson's serene look. Suddenly, on the previous day, he told Hawkins, as he was praying, he was relieved of the dropsy. "It is wonderful," he exclaimed, "very wonderful."

He was still too weak to leave his room, and the fears and misery which the relief accorded to his prayers had dispersed for a time returned. Two months later he wrote to Taylor:

"What can be the reason that I hear nothing from you? I hope nothing disables you from writing. What I have seen, and what I have felt, gives me reason to fear everything. Do not omit giving me the comfort of knowing, that after all my losses I have yet a friend left.

"I want every comfort. My life is very solitary and cheerless. Though it has pleased God wonderfully to deliver me from the dropsy, I am yet very weak, and have not passed the door since the thirteenth of December. I hope for some help from warm weather, which will surely come in time. . . . Oh, my friend, the approach of death is very dreadful. I am afraid to think on that which I know I cannot avoid. It is vain to look round and round for that help which cannot be had."

As the summer came on, his health improved, and he visited Oxford, taking Boswell with him. A few days after his return, on June 30, he and Boswell dined together for the last time. They drove back to Bolt Court together, and Johnson asked Boswell to come in, but Boswell, fearing to be depressed by Johnson's melancholy, declined. "We bade adieu to each other affectionately in the carriage. When he had got down upon the foot-pavement, he called out, 'Fare you well'; and without looking back, sprung away with a kind of pathetick briskness, if I may use that expression, which seemed to indicate a struggle to conceal uneasiness, and impressed me with a foreboding of our long, long separation."

The next day Johnson heard from Hester Thrale that Piozzi was returning to marry Mrs. Thrale. Johnson had corresponded with Mrs. Thrale fairly regularly throughout the previous twelve months, being still unable altogether to abandon the hope of renewing their old friendship, though he must have realized that she was staying in Bath chiefly to avoid him. "Your kind expressions gave me great pleasure," he wrote to her in March; "do not reject me from your thoughts. Shall we ever exchange confidence by the fireside again?"

When he heard about Piozzi from Hester, he replied: "I read your letter with anguish and astonishment, such as I had never felt before. I had fondly flattered myself that time had produced better thoughts. . . . You have not left your Mother, but your Mother has left you. . . . I send my kindest respects to your sisters, and exhort them to attend to your counsels, and recommend you all to the care of Him who is the Father of the fatherless."

The next day he received a circular letter which Mrs. Thrale had sent to all Thrale's executors, informing them that her three eldest daughters had left Bath for Brighton with a Miss Nicholson, having refused her company because they had heard that Mr. Piozzi was returning from Italy to marry her. With this circular she sent Johnson a letter in which she asked his pardon for concealing a connexion he must have heard of, but perhaps never believed.

"Indeed, my dear Sir, it was concealed only to save us both needless pain; I could not have borne to reject that counsel it would have killed me to take, and I only tell it you now because all is irrevocably settled, and out of your power to prevent. I will say, however, that the dread of your disapprobation has given me some anxious moments, and I feel as though acting without a parent's consent till you write kindly to—Your faithful servant."

Johnson replied:

"MADAM,—If I interpret your letter right, you are ignominiously married; if it is yet undone, let us once more talk together. If you have abandoned your children and your religion, God forgive your wickedness: if you have forfeited your fame and your country, may your folly do no further mischief. If the last act is yet to do, I who have loved you, esteemed you, reverenced you, and served you, I who long thought you the first of humankind, entreat that, before your fate is irrevocable, I may once more see you. I was, I once was,—Madam, most truly yours,

SAM. JOHNSON.

"I will come down, if you permit it."

To this letter Mrs. Thrale sent the following answer:

"SIR,—I have this morning received from you so rough a letter in reply to one which was both tenderly and respectfully written, that I am forced to desire the conclusion of a correspondence which I can bear to continue no longer. The birth of my second husband is not meaner than that of my first; his sentiments are not meaner; his profession is not meaner, and his superiority in what he professes acknowledged by all mankind. It is want of fortune then that is ignominious; the character of the man I have chosen has no other claim to such an epithet. The religion to which he has always been a zealous adherent will, I hope, teach him to forgive insults he has not deserved; mine will, I hope, enable me to bear them at once with dignity and patience. To hear that I have forfeited my fame is indeed the greatest insult I ever yet received. My fame is as unsullied as snow, or I should think it unworthy of him who is henceforth to protect it.

"I write by the coach the more speedily and effectually to prevent your coming hither. Perhaps by my fame (and I hope it is so) you mean only that celebrity which is a consideration of a much lower kind. I care for that only as it may give pleasure to my husband and his friends.

"Farewell, dear Sir, and accept my best wishes. You have always commanded my esteem, and long enjoyed the fruits of a friendship never infringed by one harsh expression on my part during twenty years of familiar talk. Never did I oppose your will, or control your wish; nor can your unmerited severity itself lessen my regard; but till you have changed your opinion of Mr. Piozzi let us converse no more. God bless you."

Whether Johnson received this letter in an interval of calm, or was composed by its dignity and absence of recrimination, he replied very tenderly:

"DEAR MADAM,—What you have done, however I may lament it, I have no pretence to resent, as it has not been injurious to me: I therefore breathe out one sigh more of tenderness, perhaps useless, but at least sincere.

"I wish that God may grant you every blessing, that you may be happy in this world for its short continuance, and eternally happy in a better state; and whatever I can contribute to your happiness I am very ready to repay, for that kindness which soothed twenty years of a life radically wretched.

"Do not think slightly of the advice which I now presume to

offer. Prevail upon Mr. Piozzi to settle in England: you may live here with more dignity than in Italy, and with more security: your rank will be higher, and your fortune more under your own eye. I desire not to detail all my reasons, but every argument of prudence and interest is for England, and only some phantoms of imagination seduce you to Italy.

"I am afraid, however, that my counsel is vain, yet I have eased my heart by giving it.

"When Queen Mary took the resolution of sheltering herself in England, the Archbishop of St. Andrew's, attempting to dissuade her, attended on her journey; and when they came to the irremeable stream that separated the two kingdoms, walked by her side into the water, in the middle of which he seized her bridle, and with earnestness proportioned to her danger and his own affection pressed her to return. The Queen went forward— If the parallel reaches thus far, may it go no further. The tears stand in my eyes.

"I am going into Derbyshire, and hope to be followed by your good wishes, for I am, with great affection,—Your, etc.,

"SAM. JOHNSON."

His comparison of her journey to Italy and the flight of Mary to England, with its sequel of imprisonment and execution, bore no relation to reality. The general outcry against Mrs. Thrale's marriage made it necessary for her to leave England; and she naturally chose Italy to go to, both for its own sake and as the country of her husband. Had Piozzi held her to ransom in a cave in the Apennines, as seems to have been expected by her London friends, and is implicitly foretold in Johnson's historical parallel, Johnson's advice would have been timely. But Piozzi did not turn into a brigand on crossing the Italian frontier. He remained what he had been before, gentle, affectionate, and well-conducted, and his wife's happiness was still further increased by his countrymen, in Milan, Florence, and elsewhere, who gave her a social triumph which made up to her for what she had for the time being lost in England.

In her reply to Johnson, recently published for the first time by Mr. Tyson and Mr. Guppy, she tried to persuade him that her journey to Italy was reasonable.

"Not only my good Wishes but most fervent Prayers for your Health and Consolation shall for ever attend and follow my dear Mr. Johnson. Your last letter is sweetly kind, and I thank you for it most sincerely. Have no Fears for me, however; no *real* Fears. My Piozzi will need few Perswasions to settle in a Country where he has succeeded so well; but he longs to shew me to his Italian Friends, and he wishes to restore my Health by treating me with a Journey to many Places I have long wish'd to see. . . . He is a religious Man, a sober Man, a Thinking Man—he will not injure me, I am sure he will not, let nobody injure him in your good Opinion, which he is most solicitous to obtain and preserve, and the harsh Letter you wrote to me at first grieved him to the very heart. Accept his Esteem, my dear Sir, do; and his Promise to treat with long continued Respect and Tenderness the Friend whom you once honoured with your Regard and who will never cease to be, my dear Sir,
Your truly affectionate and faithful serv^t."

The rage of the old man flared up again when he read this letter, the signature to which he violently erased. His self-control had been sapped by the strain of the previous three years, and his rage was the revolt, suppressed through a long life of misery, against the exclusion from happiness to which his mental and physical infirmities had condemned him. Everything which he had missed was symbolized to him in the picture of Mrs. Thrale in Italy with her lover. Her letter was tender and respectful, but no malice could have hurt him so much as the ignorance of his feelings which allowed her to write: "He wishes to restore my Health by treating me with a Journey to many Places I have long wish'd to see."

His anger against life, masked as disgust with Mrs. Thrale, fastened its hold on him. "I love you," he wrote to Hester Thrale a few weeks later, "I loved your Father, and I loved your Mother as long as I could." Public opinion, he continued, was always worthy of great attention; such practices could very seldom be right which all the world had concluded to be wrong. Four years after he wrote this, Mrs. Piozzi was again in Bath, surrounded by the admiring attention of the public which four years earlier had driven her out of England.

As the autumn approached, his asthma became severe again, and his dropsy returned. He visited his old haunts for the last time: Ashbourne, Lichfield, Birmingham, and Oxford. At Lichfield, Anna Seward relates, he spoke of Mrs. Thrale as a being without veracity or worth of any kind. "The great Johnson is here," she wrote to a friend on October 29, "labouring under the paroxysms of a disease, which must speedily be fatal. He shrinks from the consciousness with the extremest horror." She visited him often, she continues, though conscious that he had small regard for her, and was anxious only to forget in any society his terror of the approaching end.

One day she called at Lucy Porter's to take tea with him, and found him in an arm-chair in deep but agitated slumber. "I stood by him several minutes," the stout and sentimental Anna records, "mournfully contemplating the temporary suspension of those vast intellectual powers, which must so soon, as to *this* world, be eternally quenched."

The servant entered to announce a visitor, and Johnson, awaking with convulsive starts, got to his feet with an alacrity which surprised Anna, but may be explained by his realization that he had been lying at the mercy of her melting regard. "Come, my dear lady," he exclaimed, "let you and I attend these gentlemen in the study."

Salutations exchanged, Johnson seated himself astride a chair, his face to its back, and keeping up a trotting motion as if on horseback poured forth a stream of eloquence, illuminated by frequent flashes of wit and humour.

From Lichfield Johnson went to Birmingham, where he spent a few days with Edmund Hector, whom he begged to put on paper all that he could remember of their early days together and send it to him. Hector complied, and his account reached Johnson a few days before his death.

He arrived in London on November 16. His dropsy increased rapidly, and thinking the town air might be the cause he went to Islington for two or three days, but as there was no improvement he returned to Bolt Court. Before setting out for Islington, he was visited by Fanny Burney, who said she had just seen Hester Thrale and asked him if he ever heard from Hester's mother. "No," he cried, "nor write to her. I drive her quite from my mind. If I meet with one of her letters, I burn it instantly. I have burnt all I can find. I never speak of her, and I desire never to hear of her more. I drive her, as I said, quite from my mind." This was his last word about the person he had loved most in the world, and to whom he had once said, "The cup of life is surely bitter enough, without squeezing in the hateful rind of resentment."

His love for the poor remained with him till the end. He

was bound to them not merely because he had shared their struggles, but also because, even when he became famous, his infirmities still excluded him, as their circumstances excluded them, from a full share in the inheritance of life. Peyton and Levett, and many others of whom we have no record, were to him fellows in affliction, not the uncouth objects of a great man's bounty.

More than two-thirds of his pension had been given away each year, but when, a fortnight before his death, he yielded to Hawkins's insistence, and drew up his will, he found that he was much richer than he supposed. His books had been selling for many years, and his fortune now amounted to £2300. The worldly strain in his nature made him for a short time consider bequeathing his Lichfield house to Pembroke College, but he mastered this pricking of ostentation, and left his property as follows: £200 to the representatives of Thomas Innys, a bookseller who had helped his father; £100 to a woman domestic; the proceeds on the sale of his Lichfield house to some poor and distant relations; and the remainder, in the form of an annuity, to Francis Barber. Lucy Porter, who had been left a fortune by her brother, he did not mention in his will, much to her displeasure.

The size of Francis's annuity incensed Hawkins. Johnson had asked his doctor how much he ought to give a favourite servant, and the doctor replying that noblemen generally pensioned their servants at fifty pounds a year, Johnson said, "Then I shall be nobilissimus, for I mean to leave Frank seventy pounds a year." In his life of Johnson, Hawkins, who had not expected his efforts in getting Johnson to make a will to prove so entirely disinterested, enters "a *caveat* against ostentatious bounty and favour to Negroes." To indemnify himself for all his pains, he appropriated Johnson's only valuable piece of personal property, a gold watch, which Johnson had intended for Frank. The other executors forced him to disgorge his booty, Frank got the watch, and Sir John had to content himself with charging his coach hire to Johnson's estate.

The provisions of the will were settled on November 27. Calling on Johnson the next day, Hawkins found several friends with him, but Johnson himself was asleep. Presently he awoke and collecting himself said that they could see the state he was in, conflicting with bodily pain and mental distraction. Let them, while they were in health and strength, labour to do good and avoid evil, if ever they hoped to escape the distress that now oppressed him. Yet sometimes, he said, rays of hope shot into his soul, almost persuading him that he was in a state of reconciliation with God.

His horror of what might await him beyond death was intensified by his innate scepticism. In one of his last prayers he wrote: "And while it shall please Thee to continue me in this world, where much is to be done and little to be known, teach me by Thy Holy Spirit to withdraw my mind from unprofitable and dangerous inquiries, from difficulties vainly curious, and doubts impossible to be solved." The doubts which made God unreal to his intellect increased instead of lessening his terrors, because they seemed to him a sign that he was not worthy to be saved.

So far as his thoughts were still concerned with this world, they centred on those he had loved in his earlier years. In July, a few days after he had heard from Mrs. Thrale that she was marrying Piozzi, he wrote to the vicar of Bromley, where his wife was buried, saying that he wished to put a stone

upon the grave. Ten days before his death, he wrote to Lucy
Porter to tell her that he had that summer laid a stone on the
grave of her mother; and on the same day he sent a Lichfield
friend an epitaph for his father, mother, and brother, to be
engraved on a stone. "The first care," he said, "must be to
find the exact place of interment, that the stone may protect
the bodies. Let the stone be deep, massy, and hard; do not
let the difference of ten pounds, or more, defeat our purpose."

One day, shortly before his death, he burnt his mother's
letters. When they were consumed, he burst into tears, and
picked up the ashes to see if any words were still legible.

Bennet Langton visited him often towards the close, and
Burke and Reynolds came to pay their last tribute of respect
to the great spirit which had never fainted in the prison of
its corrupted body. "I am afraid, Sir," said Burke, "such a
number of us may be oppressive to you." "No, Sir, it is not
so," said Johnson; "and I must be in a wretched state, indeed,
when your company would not be a delight to me." "My dear
Sir, you have always been too good to me," Burke answered
in a trembling voice, and left the room.

The dropsy increased, and Johnson kept on begging his
physicians to make deeper incisions, both to relieve the pain
and to prolong his life. "How many men," he cried, "die
through the timidity of those whom they consult for health!
I want length of life, and you fear giving me pain, which I
care not for." On the day before his death he refused to take
any more food or medicine, feeling that it was useless to resist
the inevitable any longer. During the night the dropsy increased beyond his endurance. A friend had left a servant
with him, and Johnson forced the man to hand him a lancet.
He had concealed a pair of scissors in his bed, and with the

lancet and scissors made several deep incisions, which gave him the relief he craved. The poison which had tormented him throughout his life flowed away, and he slept tranquilly through the next day, December 13, waking once or twice to take some nourishment. At a quarter past seven, he turned to Sastres, murmured, "Jam moriturus," and breathed out his last breath without any struggle or sign of pain.

THE END

INDEX